THE
MAKING OF AMERICA
SERIES

BARDSTOWN
HOSPITALITY, HISTORY, AND BOURBON

DIXIE HIBBS

To Joe Bishop —
Hope you enjoy this book!
Dixie Hibbs
Dec 3, 2005

ARCADIA

Copyright © 2002 by Dixie Hibbs.
ISBN 0-7385-2391-7

Published by Arcadia Publishing,
an imprint of Tempus Publishing, Inc.
2 Cumberland Street
Charleston, SC 29401

Printed in Great Britain.

Library of Congress Catalog Card Number: 2002107723

For all general information contact Arcadia Publishing at:
Telephone 843-853-2070
Fax 843-853-0044
E-Mail sales@arcadiapublishing.com

For customer service and orders:
Toll-Free 1-888-313-2665

Visit us on the Internet at http://www.arcadiapublishing.com

FRONT COVER: *Brown's Mill was a local landmark used in many postcard pictures and advertisements. On Town Creek just over the hill east of town, it was a favorite site for picture taking. This 1895 photo was probably taken by local photographer W.F. Montfort. The dilapidated mill was purchased by the city in 1901 and torn down.*

CONTENTS

ACKNOWLEDGMENTS

I continue to follow in the footsteps of three noted Nelson County historians, Jack Muir, John B. Thomas, and Sarah Smith, in preserving in print the images and stories of the past. Although all are deceased, their collections continue to contribute to our understanding of local history. Mr. Muir's interest in the history of the community and his life-long habit of clipping news items allowed me to find the elusive details that straight line research fails to uncover. Mr. Thomas's research in newspapers and Civil War stories has been invaluable. He generously gave me permission to use his materials in all my writings. I also used materials from the public collections of the Kentucky Historical Society, the Sisters of Charity of Nazareth Archives, My Old Kentucky Home State Park, the Nelson County Circuit Court, and the Nelson County Historical Society. I also continued to draw from my extensive collection of photographs and original papers of local historic interest.

Over the years, many people have given me items that they wanted preserved and used. This generosity has allowed me to compile seven books about Nelson County.

No project is completed without help. My friend Mary Tipton stepped in at the last and carefully proofed all the grammar, spelling, etc. Donna Wilhite, graphic artist at *The Kentucky Standard*, has always provided advice and help with pictures.

I wish to thank my family, and my mother Christine Polley, for feeding us many nights after I had typed all day.

My husband Franklin must also be thanked for the patience with the confusion and the last minute proofreading that was essential to my peace of mind. The facts are as accurate as I could find, but, being human, I may have used the wrong reference, so please read with charity. I wish I could have stuffed every bit of historical trivia I've found into this story, but there is never enough space.

INTRODUCTION

Bardstown, Kentucky isn't a typical slow-moving, southern town. It is a progressive, historic community that began with big dreams and land speculators, and survived the ups and downs of more than two centuries. Located about 45 miles southeast of Louisville and 60 miles west of Lexington, Bardstown has a population of 10,374 as of the last census. Settled in 1780 by immigrants from Pennsylvania, Maryland, and Virginia, it would rise from the primitive wilds of western Virginia with the building of log, brick, or stone houses.

In 1785, it became the county seat of Nelson County, Virginia. In 1792, Kentucky's statehood opened up more economic opportunities for the area. Although it was called Salem by the original owners, David Bard and John C. Owings, very soon it was known as "Bard's Town."

Leaders in politics, education, religion, and commerce contributed to the growth and success of the town. Bardstown's central location on turnpikes and highways during the last 200 years brought travelers from near and far. Some stayed a short time, others never left. Those roads also brought soldiers at war and carried local draftees away, some never to return. Students came to learn and used their learning to be leaders in politics, medicine, religion, and the military. More than 2,000 young men studied at Saint Joseph College in the 1800s. Trains came and carried away the bourbon for which Kentucky is known. The bourbon-making families continued through the ups and downs of the industry. Bardstown is far enough south for southern hospitality, but also far enough north that grits aren't served with every breakfast. Bardstown hospitality is southern in flavor: "Welcome! Come on in." "Visit, or sit and stay awhile." "Come back again." Many visitors returned or, if they could not return, sent their friends and family to enjoy the Bardstown hospitality.

The following story is somewhat incomplete. It is an outline of the highlights of local history. It is meant to shape an understanding of where the town started, what trials and pains it suffered and how it overcame those and preserved the best of the past. How can you tell the entire story when you have limited space? Historic trivia overflows the research file, waiting for just the right hole in a paragraph to tell the whole story. But there are always more facts than the story can hold. Use your imagination to place the people and events in the town.

Bardstown has used its imagination more than once in the past when, through organized community effort, it succeeded in buying the house that inspired the state song of Kentucky, in producing an outdoor musical when other support failed, and in working to preserve the physical heritage of great architecture and historic buildings.

In 1967, Bardstown passed a historic zoning ordinance to protect the buildings of the community. Some historic buildings were demolished as early as the 1920s, but today, more than 300 buildings are listed on the National Register of Historic Places. But the greatest treasures of the community are the people who contributed to its welfare and growth for the last two centuries, and those who are now committed to preserving and improving it today.

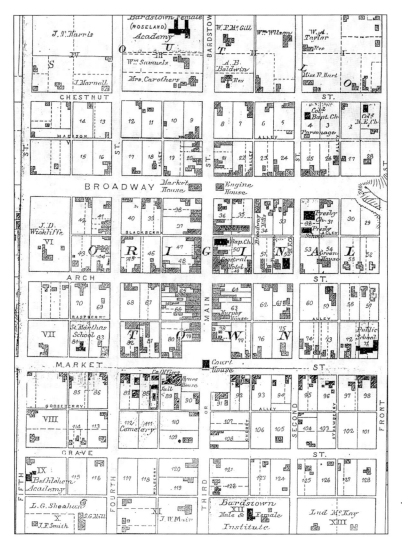

This 1882 map has been modified and the areas south of Duke and north of Beall have been omitted. In the late 1930s, the east–west street names were changed. Beall and Broadway remained the same, but Chestnut became Brashear, Arch became Flaget, Market became Stephen Foster, Graves became John Fitch, and Duke became Muir.

1. Settlement Years, 1780–1800

In the summer and fall of 1780, William Bard greeted fellow Pennsylvanians and settlers from northern Virginia as they landed on the south side of the Ohio to avoid "shooting the Falls" on flatboats. He managed his brother David's land, and he offered "free" rent to those who would come into the wilds of Kentucky and build a house 16 feet square in the planned town of 130 lots. The land was located in Jefferson County about 45 miles south of the Falls and was laid out on an elevation to provide a healthy setting with drainage away from the settlement. This free rent offer was good only while the "war was going on," the Indian War in Kentucky, which was supported by the British during the Revolutionary War. The last battle of the revolution was fought at Blue Licks in Kentucky in 1782.

Thirty-three settlers accepted the offer. They cleared the forest and erected crude brush cabins in the summer and fall of 1780, becoming the first inhabitants of what would become Bard's Town, Virginia, then in 1792, Bard's Town, Kentucky.

The first exploration of the area was by intrepid scouts from Virginia in the five years before the town was settled. They came down the river or through the Cumberland Gap following the game trails. The hunters would later be followed by the "locaters," those who were locating land for land grant holders in Virginia, Pennsylvania, and Maryland. These grants could be military warrants, issued to veterans of the French and Indian War or the provision suppliers for that war, or they were warrants issued to those who brought people into the area for settlement. These warrants were issued by the royal governors in the name of the King of England. Another grant, known as a preemption warrant, recognized the early exploration and improvement of land by the first settlers. A crude cabin, three logs high, was enough proof of ownership to defend a preemption claim. David Bard and John C. Owings had a preemption treasury warrant dated April 26, 1780 for the Bardstown land. Later grants were issued to Continental Army veterans by Virginia and other states, and were known as military grants. All of these warrants could be sold or traded and some were stolen by the unscrupulous. In fact, more land was given out in warrants than actually existed in the land area of Kentucky.

Controversy and lawsuits over land titles continued for 40 years. One example of a challenge over land ownership concerns the grandfather of President

Abraham Lincoln. Grandfather Abraham Lincoln gave his land warrant to John Reid to locate and enter a claim for him into the land entry book in the early 1780s. Reid located the land, but he wrote, "I assign this warrent to John Reid and his heirs for value received. Abraham Linkhorn" to the bottom of the paper and claimed it in his own name. The Lincolns came to Kentucky, cleared land, and built a cabin. Reid's family also settled in Kentucky. Abraham Lincoln and John Reid were both killed by Native Americans. In 1797, after discovering the forged assignment, Lincoln's heirs sued Reid's heirs for return of the title of the land. This case was typical of the time, with depositions of witnesses about conversations between Reid and Lincoln, and what had occurred. After many court delays, the final judgment in 1816 indicated that the Lincolns were entitled to the land and damages.

The 300 flatboats that ventured down the Ohio River in the spring of 1780 were filled with brave men and families that had cut their ties with the "old settlements" and were looking for fertile land and opportunity.

This was a dangerous time to settle in Kentucky. Native Americans had always been a threat as the settlers invaded their hunting grounds. Now, they were supported and supplied with weapons by the British to wait in ambush or attack scattered settlements. The winter of 1780 was so severe that animals froze in the forest. The hunting, which would supply the settlers with food until their crops were harvested, was curtailed because of the harsh winter. The rivers and buffalo traces were the easiest trails to use to travel inland in Kentucky and were heavily traveled, but not without peril. The settlement of Bardstown was never directly attacked, but fortified houses several miles outside of the town were used for defense. In 1782, an attack on Polke's Station (later called the "Burnt Station"), about 6 miles northeast of town on Simpson's Creek, resulted in the killing or kidnaping of 13 people.

But still the settlers continued to stream into Kentucky County, Virginia now, in 1780, divided into Fayette, Lincoln, and Jefferson Counties.

Named for Governor Thomas Nelson of Virginia, Nelson County was officially formed January 1, 1785. The first Gentleman Justices were appointed on May 24, 1785. Isaac Cox, Andrew Hynes, James Rogers, Angus Cameron, James Morrison, Philip Phillips, Benjamin Pope, Joseph Barrett, David Cox, Charles Polke, and Thomas Helm were justices of the peace in and for the county of Nelson. Isaac Cox would be the justice of the chancery; Samuel Smythe, sheriff; Isaac Morrison, clerk; William May, surveyor; Reverend Joseph Barnett and Reverend William Taylor, ministers; David Bland, Alexander Lasley, Joseph Bogarth, and John Smith, constables; and John Grundy, deputy sheriff.

In July 1785, the justices issued the order "that the Pillar Side of a Spanish Dollar be the seal of this county until another be provided." Spanish silver dollars were the hard money of the early Kentucky years. With ingenuity, the dollars were cut into four equal parts or quarters, worth 25¢ each, and these again were divided into eighths or 12¢ pieces. This is where the term "pieces of eight," referring to

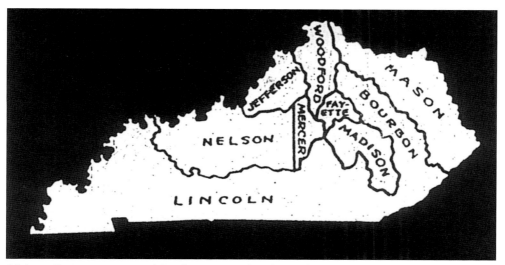

Nelson County was created by the Virginia legislature from Jefferson County in December 1784 and Bard's Town was chosen as the county seat. The county area stretched north to the Salt River, west to the Ohio River, south to the Green River, and east to the eastern edge of present Washington County.

silver coins of pirate treasure, was initiated. Most of this money came from New Orleans business transactions.

Four months after their appointment, the Gentleman Justices were hearing multiple petitions and cases of debt, trespass, assault and battery, slander, infamous gambler, trespass for scandal, and horse theft. Most of these were disagreements among individuals, but an interesting case was the charge of slander by James and Elizabeth Purcell against John and Elizabeth Carr. The jury determined that the defendants were guilty and assessed damages of 17 pounds, 1 shilling, and 10 pence, with costs. What made this interesting is an entry the next day stating that the parties had access to the jury before the verdict, the judgement was nullified, and the case was to be retried.

Another unusual case for Nelson County was the case of piracy tried in Bardstown concerning a former British soldier calling flatboats over to the bank of the Ohio River under pretense of needing help and then robbing them. This piracy occurred in 1783, but was tried in Nelson County because the Ohio River was the western boundary of the county at this time. The man went to jail.

The justices appointed surveyors of the roads, who could call on the citizens along the byways to labor on the roads. The surveyor was to serve two years and was directed to see that the roads were cleared, ditched, and in good repair. All males over 16 and under 50 years of age, except licensed ministers of the gospel, were assigned to work on some road. If the worker failed to attend the day assigned, without sending a substitute, he could be fined $1.25 per time. The surveyor was also to set up, at the forks or crossing of every public road, an index

11

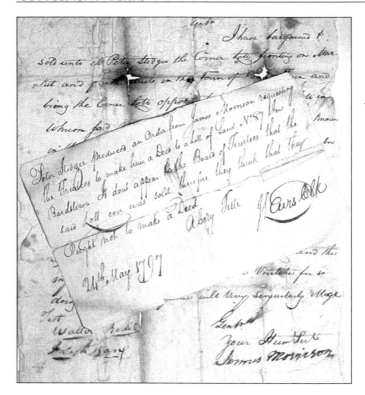

A bill of sale to Peter Stidger from James Morrison for Lot #87 shows the complications faced by the trustees. A request to make a deed of the land, "formerly claimed by Young Ewing, then sold to me, and I sold to Peter Stidger." The trustee's reply is that the lot was never sold.

with plain inscriptions in large letters directing to the most noted place that each road led. Anyone destroying or defacing these signs, or "finger boards," was fined $10 for each offense. In 1796, the county released the Bardstown males from working on any public roads if they assisted in repairing the streets of the town.

As the county seat for a large area, the town grew to accommodate the many citizens traveling to record deeds, file lawsuits, and register official papers. All official court papers and cases were held at the courthouse in Bardstown. Marriages, wills, deeds, powers of attorney, indictments of lawbreakers, lawsuits, tax collection, and militia returns had to be filed at the county seat. The Court of Quarter Sessions would meet every quarter for the prosecution of crimes and the settling of disputes. The county court met once a month.

William Bard misplaced his papers of the town's earliest years, but he was able to create these documents from memory to be recorded. In *Deed Book 7*, on page 211, the following is recorded:

> ADVERTISEMENT FEBY. 11TH 1782
> Whereas it apears to the inhabitants that Jefferson County requires to be divided and that the new town called Salem is Centrical for a Courthouse; therefore the following term is proposed. Viz in lots contained one quarter of an acre with an out lot containing three acres

and only a quit rent of two silver dollars per year to be paid to the propriater, thereof good titles will be given on Demand after David Bard obtains his premption Pattant for the same. The whole cleer of rent during the Disturbance by the present Indian War in these parts, and until the out lots is properly laid off after the war, Setlars may clear as much ajacent land, as is necessay for the support of their families; and those geting by lottery the clear land in their out lots shall pay the value of the improvements or cleear as much to him that made it—Setlars on their in lots who build a house at least sixteen feet square and cleers off the underbrush, shall have a right to their lots. Wm. for David Bard

The above is a true coppy of the substance of the first terms or advertisement which was mislead or stole before I coppyed it, any other way than by memory. Certify—By William Bard

Salem Town March 10th 1784

This is to give notice that all the outlots which I mean to give are already taken. Those wanting in lots in future may only obtain a right to them by agreeement under hand write from the Subscriber. Those having complement of cleer land ajoinin the town may make use of the same agreeable to the Custom of the country until it pays them for cleering the outlots. I expect will be laid off this summer or fall and as the abuse of timber may in time be felt by the inhabitants of this Town, I request that none may kill or cut any green Timber unless for a building by Consent of their Humble Servt. Wm. Bard

Three years later, this announcement of sales of inlots indicated there were still some problems remaining in the titles:

I, William Bard, being about to dispose of a number of unappropriated lots in Bards Town hath determined on the following Terms & Regulations which are to be observed by all Persons becoming Purchasers viz: any Person purchasing a Lot or Lots, are to improve the Same by building in eighteen months thereon, a house of Brick, Stone or frame sixteen feet square with a stone or brick chimney thereto or forfeit the said lots, which are to be paid for at the average price of the Lots sold at publick sale on Bard & Fourth Streets, for which the said Lots are reserved. The Lots on Arch Street are not to be disposed of by the present agents, without further instructions—Any Quarter in lots are not be disposed of by the agents that shall be adjoining the Thirty Three first settlers or laid off in quarter Lots, or any other lot already settled on. Mr. Charles Ewing, George & Cuthbert Harrison, are hereby empowered to let the lots intended to be disposed of agreeable to the above regulations & Each person taking a Lot to pay Mr. Charles Ewing two shilling and six pence for laying of Each Lot. Wm. Bard, October 6th, 1785, a copy of the original by G. Harrison.

The land grant giving David Bard and John C. Owings ownership of the land was issued July 21, 1785 with the description, ". . . containing one thousand acres by survey bearing date of 20th day of March 1784 lying and being in the county of Jefferson including Bardstown."

David Bard was a Pennsylvanian minister who never lived in Kentucky. His affairs were handled by his brother William, who chose the town site, laid off the lots, and promoted the site to the settlers from the east. Owings never came to Kentucky either, but his son Thomas D. Owings was an active land speculator in central Kentucky.

Bardstown was laid off in 1781, according to county records. Various spellings of the name—Bard's Town, Baird's Town, Beardstown—are found in the early papers, but the Bard family name was the correct spelling.

In a deposition in the *Land Causes* book, Proctor Ballard testifies "that on the 18th day of March 1782, I moved to Bardstown which was then called Salem and Conrad Curtz moved the same spring and settled on the two 1/4 acre lots now in contention." After a petition was sent to the Virginia legislature, the town was incorporated on December 12, 1788, and its administration was placed in a board of trustees. One of their first recorded acts in the early fall of 1789 was to appoint a surveyor, George Calhoun, and order a survey of the 130 one-half-acre lots. He was to establish the dimensions of the streets and alleys. The trustees stipulated that Spring Street, later called Main, now Broadway, should be 132 feet wide. Other streets, such as Second, were laid between buildings already constructed, causing them to be the narrowest streets in town. This plat was recorded in *Deed Book 5*, page 340 in July 1797, and is still used.

The trustees then advertised and auctioned, on October 30, 1789, all the unclaimed lots as surveyed. Buyers bought single lots or as many as 13, as 110 lots were sold. The original 33 settlers were acknowledged as lot owners of at least 20 lots, which were not sold. Most of these (14) were along Market Street extending from just west of the town square and then two blocks east. Signing the first deed on November 12 were the trustees, Isaac Morrison, Walter Beall, James Baird, John Reed, Andrew Hynes, Phillip Phillips, John Caldwell, Gabriel Cox, James Adams, Thomas Morton, and Michael Campbell.

Lots #111 and #112 at the corner of Fourth and Graves Streets were set aside for a public graveyard. It is probable they had already been used for that purpose before the auction. Concerned about pollution of water supplies, in 1819, the trustees ruled that no one could be buried within the town except on the "jail lot," the above two lots. "All other burials had to be in the graveyard outside of town," probably referring to the Presbyterian Cemetery on the northeast corner of the preemption.

Notice was given on June 10, 1795 that all the old cabins and other nuisances on Market Street be removed. Many of these were erected before the street and lot lines were staked and interfered with the plan.

Early concerns of the trustees were the locations of the buildings. They set up rules that determined that no house could be built within 50 feet of a neighbor's house, kitchen, or store of hay fodder or straw. Later, in 1817, they prohibited the building of stables, pig pens, cow lots, or barns within 75 feet of the street and noted that the buildings should be farther away if possible.

In 1785, the Gentleman Justices determined that the best place for the public buildings in Nelson County was "in the square in the South Street of Baird's Town," which is the 2 acres of ground sold by William Bard to the county for 5 shillings. In 1785, the court specified in detail the building of two jails: a debtor's prison 15 feet square built of "square loggs a foot thick" and the criminals' prison, to be 10 feet square with "square loggs a foot thick to be planked inside and out, the planks to be four inches thick." These buildings were erected on the public square along with stocks, pillory, and stray pen. The stocks and pillory were used to punish minor crimes, such as petty theft, malicious gossip, and breach of peace. The stray pen was necessary to contain stray livestock brought to town by travelers. Livestock owners could claim them by identifying them and paying for their keep to the sheriff. Richard McMahan was noted in the records as receiving payment for building a "gaol" before 1788, and Walter Beall was paid 292 pounds for a jail built by November 1789. The debtor's jail was built by March 1789.

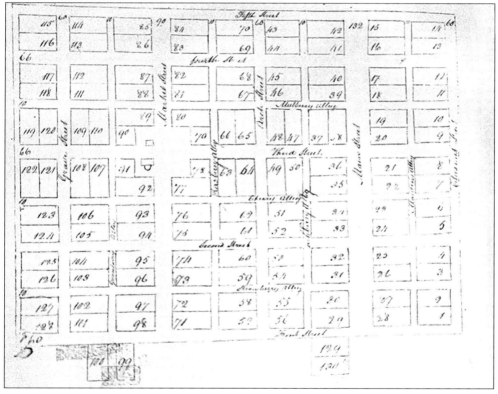

In the early fall of 1789, the trustees appointed a surveyor, George Calhoun, and ordered a survey of the 130 one-half-acre lots. He was to establish the dimensions of the streets and alleys. This plat was recorded in Deed Book 5 *in July 1797 and is still used.*

Meanwhile, the erection of a courthouse was foremost in the justices' minds. They specified the details and contracted with John Cape to design and construct a building. He also designed and constructed courthouses for Fayette and Jefferson Counties during this time. The first design was a rectangle shape, but the final building was a square, two-story stone structure. Begun some time after 1788, it was not completed until 1800. A controversy over the construction and cost held up the completion.

The first census of Bard's Town, Virginia in 1790 noted a population of 216, 16 more than Louisville, and 66 more than Danville. Two years later, on June 1, 1792, the state of Kentucky was created from western Virginia and Frankfort was chosen as the capitol city.

In 1794, the first post office in the county was opened by Postmaster Ben Grayson at Bardstown. It was soon followed by others in Bloomfield in 1803, Fairfield in 1818, and Rolling Fork in southern Nelson County in 1824. New Haven in 1829, Boston in 1831, and Chaplin in 1832 spread out the county sites where you could send and receive mail. At this time, the mail was brought by carriers on horseback to the offices. Later, after the turnpikes were constructed in the 1830s, stagecoaches carried the mail bags.

Taverns or ordinaries were built, and their owners licensed by the county. These buildings served as restaurants, hotels, meeting areas, and "watering holes."

This stone courthouse, built between 1788 and 1800, has been the scene of political and religious debates, as well as outstanding legal battles.

Virginia "common law" controlled ordinary barter and trade, and provided that the county courts would oversee and regulate public feeding and housing. As soon as the Nelson County court was organized, on June 29, 1785, three applications were received to keep an "ordinary," the contemporary term applied to a commercial establishment that provided food and lodging. It is likely that these first tavern keepers had already been in business under the jurisdiction of the Jefferson County court.

The applicant signed a 50-pound bond with a personal security to do the following:

> constantly find and provide in said ordinary, good wholesome and cleanly diet and lodging for travelers and stablage, fodder and provender or pasturage for their horses . . . shall not suffer or permit any unlawful family . . . nor on the Sabbath day suffer any person to tipple and drink more than is necessary.

The court was also responsible for setting maximum fees for everything from lodging, meals, and pasturage for the horse, to brandy, wine, and whisky per half-pint for the traveler.

The first tavern licenses were issued to Israel Dodge in his house in Bard's Town and Elizabeth Grundy at her house in Bard's Town. These licenses were to be renewed yearly, but may not have been strictly enforced. The "selling of spiritous liquors without a license" was a crime for which many were indicted. If you did not hold a license, your prices were not controlled or guaranteed and you were not in compliance with the law.

On May 3, 1793, the *Kentucky Gazette* advertised that Benjamin Frye opened a house of entertainment in Bard's Town at the sign of the Faithful Wittness. This was located on the north side of East Market (Lot #76). In the January 1, 1795 issue, James Crutcher announced that he opened a tavern in the stone house at the sign of the eagle on the southwest corner of Second and Arch Streets (Lot #61). Colonel Joseph Lewis was operating this tavern in 1797 when the owners of the lot, Thomas and John Speed, advertised it for sale.

Other tavern owners were Colonel Joseph Bane, operating on east Arch Street (Lot #54) from 1794 to 1797; Duncan McLean, operating at his dwelling house in 1798; Frye's old tavern; Joshua Wilson, operating at his dwelling house on the southwest corner of Market and Second in 1799; and Michael Couchman, operating at his dwelling house in 1797.

The first citizens of Bardstown built houses, raised gardens, and started businesses. They were also alert to the Native American threat as they traveled outside of the town. Rough brush cabins were replaced with hewed-log houses erected and finished with clapboard, many of which still stand 200 years later. Three stone houses and about 50 log buildings were noted by a visitor in 1788. Brick houses were being erected in about 1796 and 1797. The first brick house was built on the southeast corner of Chestnut (Brashear) and Third Street by

George Parke in 1796. The next was the Samuel Horine home on the southwest corner of Arch (Flaget) and Fourth, *c.* 1797. Kentucky clay for making brick became the building material of choice.

In 1788, there was a tan yard operated by Samuel Horine and Jacob Ambrose adjoining the town spring. These men were shoemakers and leather workers. Twenty years later, Benjamin Doom would operate a large tan yard on town creek below the spring, directly east of the town.

Mills were built on the streams around the area, serving the farmers and later the distillers.

A petition to the Virginia legislature dated October 24, 1789, asks for an act to establish a warehouse and site for the inspection of tobacco at or near the mouth of Stewart's Creek on the north side of the Beech Fork River: "There is a large and extensive settlement around the place. The Beech Fork is navigable for large boats as high up as this place and it is within a mile of Bairdstown." Virginia taxes could be paid in tobacco at this time with the hogsheads of leaf brought to a central warehouse.

Tanners, millers, carpenters, shoemakers, coppersmiths, blacksmiths, potters, weavers, and wheelwrights practiced their skills in the town. The county court contracted with craftsmen to take apprentices, usually young orphan children. These contracts provide early records of the occupations of many of the leading manufacturers in the area. Jacob Yoder advertised in the *Kentucky Gazette* in March 1792 "of a runaway apprentice for the hatting business. Robert Forsith about 19-20 years old." William King was a wheelwright in 1793; John Ricks was a wheelwright in 1798; Zacharias Une was a joiner and cabinetmaker in 1791; John Ducker was a taylor in 1795; Anthony Geoghagen was a taylor in 1798; and William Chineworth was a tanner in 1795—all took apprentices.

In January 1790, Bridget Roberts and Jacob Green were charged with setting fire to the public jail with the intention to destroy it. This jail was of log and was located in the square. The offenders were convicted of Breach of Peace and sentenced to jail, but Roberts submitted herself to the mercy of the court, was sentenced, and received five lashes on her bare back at the public whipping post, or pillory. County records indicate that repairs were made to the gaol, probably because of the fire.

In May 1797, the Nelson County order book recorded that the sheriff was to collect from each tithable 4 shillings, 9 pence in addition to the levy laid in the prior November for the direct purpose of building a good and sufficient jail, stray pen, and stocks, plus repairing the old jail. These were to be erected on the court square of 2 acres, which had been deeded for that purpose. Christian Hahn was to be paid $30 for building the stocks and the stray pen on the public ground.

Justices were ordered to contract and superintend the building of a good and sufficient jail for the use of the different courts, which were to sit in Bardstown. They were to choose the spot and supervise the construction. The committee appointed to "fix on the most proper place to erect the District & County Jail for the Bardstown District" reported that they had chosen the back half of Lot #88.

The first brick house in Bardstown was built in 1796 for George Parke on Lot #8, the southeast corner of Chestnut and Third Street. It was demolished to build a service station in 1926.

They purchased the east half of the lot from Matthias Weller. No descriptions or details are available about this building except that John Weller Sr. was the "undertaker" and the payment of 799 pounds, 19 shillings, and 11 pence was recorded to him.

The Nelson County Court of 1800 struggled to lease the surplus jail on the court square, but when this didn't work, they sold the building, with the buyer removing it from the square. The minutes of the Supreme Court of the Bardstown district indicate that a "sufficient jail" was accepted by the court for use in September 1798. The order reads "that the prisoner now confined in the county jail be removed to the said District Jail." This building was still in use when the next jail contract was signed *c.* 1820.

John Bowling contracted to build a new jail for $5,000 sometime between November 1819 and March 1820. A list of building expenses shows that David Keely and William Crawford together furnished 738 perches of stone; Samuel Hahn furnished 4 tons of iron and did the blacksmith work; W. Hahn did the painting and supplied the paint; and Keely also furnished two sets of stone steps, as well as twelve "cills" for under the doors and windows. Alexander Moore and John Rogers billed $1,009.33 for carpentry work. This list was submitted to the court by James Green, father-in-law of John Bowling. Bowling became ill soon after starting this jail and died in September 1820. Green finished the building and discovered that the total cost of the new jail would exceed the contract by $2,480. He submitted a petition signed by 182 citizens of Nelson County asking the court to pay for all the expenses. The records do not indicate if the court agreed to this, but it was an interesting appeal.

The 1820 jail building is a rectangle with exterior stone walls approximately 3 feet thick. The interior is divided by a stone wall running lengthwise, creating a 10-foot-wide hallway. Three rooms open behind the hallway, each approximately 16 feet by 19 feet. The second floor is identical to the first.

Some of the first settlers and property owners of the area became religious leaders, such as James Rogers, William Taylor, and Joseph Barnett, but others chose to travel from place to place preaching the gospel, such as Terah Templin. Templin, an itinerant Presbyterian minister, received a license to perform marriages in 1785. A 1786 listing of the congregation known as "Salem" may have referred to one at Bardstown, as the town was called Salem in the early years. He died on October 6, 1818 at the age of 76 and was buried at the old Presbyterian Cemetery.

Between May and November 1785, Baptist ministers Joseph Barnett and William Taylor were licensed to perform marriages, as was James Rogers in "regular communion with the Baptist Church," who was granted a license in 1793. Archibald Cameron, a Presbyterian, received a license three years later. Reverend Stephen T. Badin of the Catholic church conducted services at the log chapel in the cemetery north of town in 1798. In bad weather, services were held in homes.

Education was also sought by parents for their children even during this time when the danger of Native American attacks was still present. It would be after the Battle of Fallen Timbers in 1794 before Kentucky felt safe from these types of depredations. Two schools are mentioned in the records of this time without noting the location: John Moore was mentioned as a school master at Bardstown in 1785 and Mr. Shackleford taught the classics at his Bardstown school in 1786.

The most famous school of the period was Salem Academy. It was incorporated by Virginia in 1788 with John Caldwell, Andrew Hynes, Isaac Morrison, Terah Templin, Matthew Walton, George Harrison, John Steele, Philip Phillips, Walter Beall, James Baird, Joseph Barnett, James Morrison, James Allen, Cuthbert Harrison, and William Taylor listed as trustees. An advertisement in the *Kentucky Gazette* of Lexington, in 1791, noted the pioneer educator Dr. James Priestly as teacher. One class in this school was noted to have Joseph H. Daviess, John Rowan, Felix Grundy, Archibald Cameron, John Pope, and John Allen, all of whom became leaders in their fields. Where the first school building was located is unknown, but in 1798, a lottery was authorized for a new school building to be erected on property Walter Beall donated northeast of the town.

Nelson County native Archibald Cameron, at the age of 19, professed religion and connected himself with the Presbyterian Church at Bardstown *c.* 1789. He later laid the foundation of Presbyterians in central Kentucky.

In the last years of the 1790s, a depressed man aimlessly wandered the streets of Bardstown. Called "Poor John Fitch," few knew of his invention, which would change river navigation and open up the Louisiana Purchase. John Fitch was a surveyor who came to the western waters in 1780. He surveyed the lands of George Hart and William Coomes directly east of town, and he may have surveyed the Bardstown Preemption. He filed claims on land on Cox's Creek and Simpson's Creek. Captured by Native Americans in 1782 and taken to Canada, he escaped and went back to Pennsylvania. He was the first to use steam to power a

This original cell of the 1820 stone jail building was lined with solid wood timbers placed over the stone walls. The insert is the iron ring and staple in the center of the room where prisoners would be shackled with an iron band around their ankle and a short chain attached to the ring.

boat, operating his successful invention on the Delaware River in 1788. From May until September, the boat carried passengers between 200 and 300 miles—more efficiently than Fulton's would in 1807. Congress granted Fitch a patent for this invention in 1791. After unsuccessfully searching for funding in Washington and France, he returned to Bardstown in 1795 and died three years later. The discouraged man died at Alexander McCown's house on the southwest corner of Third and Broadway, and was buried in the public graveyard on south Fourth Street. Later investigation of the boats built by Robert Livingston and Robert Fulton proved that they were substantially the same in design as the one patented by Fitch.

With no local paper, the news was reported by the *Kentucky Gazette* of Lexington, which announced a horse race in 1797.

> Oct. 4, 1797—Bairdstown Races—Will commence on the third Weds in Oct. next and will continue Thursday and Friday free for any horse, mare or gelding, the first day, the three mile heats, second day two mile heats, and the last day one mile heat. There is one hundred and fifty dollars subscribed now. The rules of the Jockey Club of this state are to be observed in these races.

The *Kentucky Gazette*, published by John Bradford, was the first newspaper in the state. In 1796, Postmaster Ben Grayson acted as agent for the *Kentucky Gazette* and took payments and news items. Announcements of local interest and about

John Fitch designed several different boats between 1787 and 1795. This is the boat which operated on the Delaware River in 1790.

This is a 1787 copper pot still on display at the Oscar Getz Museum of Whiskey History in Bardstown. These were the type of stills made by coppersmiths and used by the first distillers in Nelson County.

local people concerning business, mail waiting at the Lexington post office, stray animals found, runaway apprentices, marriages, and crimes were printed in this paper until the first Bardstown paper was published in 1803.

In the 1790s in Kentucky, if you had a pot still and the apparatus for distilling the mash, you had a distillery. Kentucky's fertile soil and pure limestone water would provide the Pennsylvania settlers with the ingredients to produce whiskey. Corn was the dominant grain and made the difference between Kentucky and Pennsylvania products.

The federal government passed a Whiskey Tax in 1791. (They continued to increase this tax in 1802, 1814, and 1817.) This unpopular assessment was the cause of a revolt by Pennsylvania farmers known as the Whiskey Rebellion. There was also a Whiskey Rebellion in Kentucky, but it was covered up at the time and has remained hidden ever since in government archives. Colonel Thomas Marshall wrote letters to treasury officials, describing the situation in Kentucky. He wrote that he had refused one resignation (of collector) because "no other person worthy of trust living in Nelson could be got to accept the job," a comment which indicates that opposition to the law transcended political loyalties because Nelson County was a center of Federalist sentiment. He also published, in the *Kentucky Gazette* in 1794, names of those distillers who had registered their stills or distilleries. Anthony Thompson was the only Nelson County name listed.

In 1794, Kentuckians were told to register their stills and pay duties on the whiskey they were making. By 1795, the federal administration had a private treaty with leading Kentucky distillers, forgiving duties before 1794 with their promise to comply with internal revenue acts. The duty on whiskey was 54¢ per gallon still per year. If a farmer owned only one still that did not exceed 50 gallons, he was exempt from paying any tax. There is some indication that stills were taxed according to where they were located in the town or county. Later, a charge of 7¢ a gallon for finished product was collected. The penalty for not paying the tax was $250 and forfeiture of the still.

Bardstown was the destination of many travelers in the eighteenth century, but none caused more comment for the next 200 years than the Duc de Orleans and his brothers. The Duke of Orleans, Louis-Phillipe, visited Kentucky in the spring of 1797. He sailed from France in the fall of 1796 with only his servant Beaudoin for company. In order to free his brothers—the Duc de Montpensier, aged 22, and the Comte De Beaujolais, 17—from imprisonment in France, Louis-Philllipe had agreed to come to the United States.

In March 1797, his brothers having joined him, they decided to explore the frontier by following an itinerary prepared by General George Washington when they visited him at Mount Vernon. Their travel diary reveals their impressions of the scenery and people as they rode horseback through Virginia, North Carolina, Tennessee, and Kentucky. The Kentucky entries indicate that they left Nashville on May 13, and reached "Mr. Hodgin's Place" (now Hodgenville, Larue County) on May 18. Various comparison observations were made about the soil, waterways, and forests of the plateau they left with the river valley or "bottom land" they were discovering.

After dark on the evening of the 18th, they arrived at "Capt. Beens" house in "Beardstown." This East Arch Street tavern was operated until 1796 by Gabriel Cox and then sold to Captain Joseph Bayne (or Bane), who continued to operate it until his death in 1809. They spent two days there repairing their equipment and resting their horses. They also took this opportunity to bring their diaries up to date. On the morning of May 21, they left, traveling toward Louisville. At the ford of Salt River, an entry notes a description of the canoe that was used to cross the flooded river. This entry is followed by a story concerning the Bardstown visit. The duke described a marionette performance and related his impressions to the party. The host family, Captain Bane's, was enthusiastic about the entertainment and considered it an event to remember to their old age. "How little these local folk know of the world" was Philippe's entry. This was the last page of the 203-page account.

The other diaries that were kept to the end of the journey at Philadelphia were lost. In later years, the Duke of Orleans related stories of this journey from Louisville to Lexington, then to Zanesville, Ohio to Pittsburgh, Buffalo, New York, and Philadelphia. In 1799, they had contact in Havana, Cuba with one who would become a Bardstown resident ten years later. Father Benedict Joseph Flaget was teaching in Havana and was asked to convey a collection of funds from the Spanish citizens to the royal brothers. They had been delayed in Cuba for 18 months and their funds were depleted. This action by Flaget has been used to justify claims that a grateful Louis Phillipe donated paintings to the Bardstown Cathedral that Flaget built in 1816; he actually gave vestments used in the church and laboratory equipment used in Saint Joseph College. He returned to Europe and reigned as King of France from 1830 until 1848.

One of the early leaders of Bardstown was Colonel Andrew Hynes. He was appointed one of the commissioners and judges of the first Nelson County court. He was a lieutenant colonel and then colonel of the Nelson County militia. He represented Nelson County in the Virginia legislature and was a member of the Constitutional Convention of Kentucky, which prepared Kentucky for statehood in 1792. He was also active in the affairs of Bardstown and Salem Academy.

In 1796, Colonel Hynes entered into a business of merchandising goods brought from Baltimore. He hired his nephew William Rose Hynes as clerk to operate the business. In 1797, the firm Andrew and William Rose (A&WR) Hynes was formed. Later documents indicate that the profits were small as sales were made principally for salt, "generally on credit to waggoners, wood choppers, kettle tenders and the like at Bullitts Lick. . . . whereby a number of bad debts were produced." Goods were brought from Baltimore twice yearly, totaling goods equal to $23,000 in seven shipments in three years. It is thought that these goods were sold at the stone building on the court square owned by W.R. Hynes and later rented in the 1820s as a tavern house to several tavern keepers. Andrew Hynes's death in 1800 resulted in the closing of the partnership, but W.R. Hynes would continue to operate merchandising businesses and deal with his uncle's affairs as the administrator of his estate.

This engraving of the Duc of Orleans was taken from Diary of My Travels in America *by Louis-Philippe, King of France, 1830–1848.*

25

2. Years of Influence, 1800–1840

The first 40 years of the nineteenth century were years of influence for Bardstown. Political, cultural, educational, and economic leadership was provided by leading citizens of the town. The Bardstown Bar of lawyers was active in state and national government. Religious growth resulted in the erection of new churches and a Catholic cathedral that was the first in the west. Craftsmen, distillers, tanneries, and ropewalks provided goods for exporting to other states. Classical schools for girls and boys were built at this time and continued for many years. The title of "Athens of the West" was based on this period in Bardstown's history.

During the second year of the new century, a tragic event occurred—the effects are still remembered. On January 29, 1801, Dr. James Chambers and John Rowan, attorney, sat down at a table at Duncan McLean's Tavern on East Market with John Crozier and two other men. After a few beers, which Rowan had first determined not to drink, but succumbed to the temptation, and a few games of whist, Chambers tired of that game and invited Rowan to play Vigutun (21) for money. Rowan had earlier determined not to play for money, but, full of beer, he agreed. After a few hands of cards, an argument broke out. Some say it was a disagreement over each's ability to speak the dead languages of Latin and Greek, but others state that Rowan was making derogatory remarks about Dr. Chambers's father-in-law, Judge Sebastian of Frankfort. In the heat of anger, Chambers grabbed Rowan by the collar and was struck by Rowan. Insulting remarks flew back and forth, erratic blows were exchanged, and separated by others, the two unsteady foes went home.

Two days later, Dr. Chambers sent a challenge to Rowan to meet him on the field of honor. Rowan accepted and asked George M. Bibb to be his second. Major John Bullock, serving as Chambers's second, tried to block the duel, but Bibb demanded that Chambers had to withdraw his challenge. On February 3, a foggy morning down by the Beech Fork River, the two groups met. Rowan brought the dueling pistols and Bullock selected one for Dr. Chambers. After reviewing the rules, the two combatants walked off the paces, turned, and fired. They both missed. Bullock again proposed a settling of the affair, but Bibb refused. The second attempt resulted in Rowan's bullet striking Chambers in the chest. Rowan

This exhibit in the Bardstown Historical Museum shows dueling pistols, playing cards and box, and a painting representing the Rowan and Chambers duel. The letter on the right is Rowan's account of the affair.

apologized and offered his carriage to transport the wounded Chambers to town. He died the next day, requesting that Rowan not be prosecuted for his death.

Chambers's friends and angry townsmen went to Federal Hill to capture Rowan. Rowan dressed one of his servants in his hat and cloak and sent him riding away from the house, while he hid out in the woods of the plantation, but he soon realized that he had to deal with the situation. On his return to his home, he was arrested by the sheriff. Jacob Yoder, the owner of the land where the duel took place, swore out a warrant for murder. At the examining trial, testimony was heard that the duel was carried out in strict conformance to the rules of honorable dueling. Rowan was released when the presiding justice found that there was not enough evidence to carry him to the grand jury. Rowan's political enemies used this affair to try to keep him from office by passing an oath of office, which stated in part that he hadn't fought a duel, taken a challenge, or accepted a challenge for a duel with a deadly weapon. This oath is still taken 200 years later by all elected officials in Kentucky.

In 1827, Charles A. Wickliffe sold Lot #32 at the corner of Second and Broadway to the Presbyterians for $200 and free pew rent. Wickliffe never had to contribute any funds for his pew for the next 40 years of his life.

In September, another death occurred as a result of this duel. Daniel Barry, teacher at the academy, and Mr. Gilpin, silversmith, got into a violent argument over the Rowan-Chambers duel. Mr. Gilpin was killed and Barry was tried for murder. Duels weren't frequent, but it appeared that people from Bardstown used them to settle disputes as the *Kentucky Gazette* of September 20, 1808 printed that N.P. Duval was reported to have died as the result of a gun shot from a duel with L. Wilcoxson. The duel took place at Clarksville, though both men were from Bardstown.

Walter Beall was a land speculator and merchant from Baltimore who settled in Bardstown in the early years. In 1803, he advertised and sold the outlots of Bardstown to all comers. Called the "Enlargement of Bardstown," Beall traded his interest in the Bourbon Iron Furnace in Bath County to Thos D. Owings for the outlots, or the rest of the Bardstown Preemption. Owings was the son of J.C. Owings, who was an equal partner with David Bard in the ownership and development of town lots. Each original settler of an inlot received the right to a 2-acre outlot. In order for Owings to execute clear title to Beall, he had to buy or obtain a release on the outlots claimed by inlot purchasers. This was time-consuming and created a delay in Beall being able to give title to the purchasers at his auction. However, the rebuying of the outlots allowed researchers to determine where the original settled lots were located.

Beall died in 1809 and his estate still couldn't give clear titles until about 1815, though many had already commenced to build on the lots. His executors had to settle huge problems in this land swap.

In Bardstown in the summer of 1806, medical history was made when Dr. Walter Brashear, assisted by Dr. Burr Harrison, successfully removed the crushed leg of a mulatto boy at the hip. The young man's leg had been badly crushed by a barrel and the doctors determined that to save his life the leg must be taken off. He was a strong young man who had youth on his side, but it was summertime with fevers and unsanitary conditions and this had never been successfully done before. After performing the first successful hip-joint amputation in the world, Dr. Brashear practiced medicine in Lexington, then moved to Louisiana in 1822 where he died in 1860.

Good roads brought many travelers and, in September of 1805, a group of monks known as Trappists, fleeing religious restrictions in France, arrived in this area of Kentucky. They purchased land in Marion and Casey Counties, but they were unable to maintain their property and left Kentucky in 1809, returning to France after Napoleon's fall. Three lay brothers, Felix Cashot, Ignatius Hottenroth, and Peter Gates, settled in Bardstown and supported themselves in silversmithing and watchmaking. In the *Candid Review* in November 1809, the following was noted: "Anthony Sanders of Bardstown was given authority to sell all lands belonging to Rev. Urbain Guliett [leader of the Trappists] within this state—PS. I have several watches in my possession that were left with the monks for repairs. A.S."

In 1804, Walter Beall donated a new church site adjoining the Bardstown preemption to the Presbyterians. This was located on the northwest corner at the end of the present 5th Street. The deed was issued to church trustees Michael Campbell, Amos Smith, George Matthews, and John Weller, conditioned on the building of a church 36 feet by 26 feet "for the use of the Dutch and English regular ordained ministers and other members of Christ's Church." A log church is said to have been constructed and used until *c.* 1816. The lot was in use as the Presbyterian Cemetery until the mid-1800s.

Reverend Joshua L.Wilson was the first known pastor of this church, but he was only there for four years and was followed by Joseph B. Lasley in 1810. Reverend Lasley used the new Union Church (1812) for some meetings following 1816 until 1818. After a five-year span, Reverend William Scott arrived to shepherd the Presbyterians. In 1825, the congregation purchased Lot #32 and constructed a fine brick church. When Scott left in 1833, the church had grown to 121 members.

In 1833, the Reverend Nathan L. Rice arrived at this building, his first church. He later became a prominent nationally known Presbyterian clergyman and, while in Bardstown, he was a strong Protestant force. He was instrumental in the opening of the first Protestant girls' school in the west under religious sponsorship. Later known as Roseland Academy, it is thought that he was reacting to the Catholic schools and Catholic influence on the community. The Catholic schools made no distinction in taking non-Catholic students, and this was an attempt to offer a Protestant choice.

Itinerant peddler Samuel P. Jones's death in 1804 was to provide the means for the first brick church building in Bardstown. He directed in his will that "my lots 3 & 4 to be occupied for the use of a graveyard forever" and all property be sold and the proceeds be used to construct a church on the same and "all preachers that preach Jesus Christ and him crussified [sic] shall have free access to preach therein and every person that bares [sic] the name of Christian to be buried thereon if that be their wish." His executors carried out his directions and, on the 9th of May, 1811, John Weller and James Houston signed a contract to build a brick building 40 feet long and 30 feet wide. The first story was to be 10 feet high, 2 bricks thick, and the second story was to be 12 feet high and 1 brick thick. All of the work was to be done by December 25. The total cost of materials was about $1,200. By 1812, the two-story brick meeting house, now called the Union Church, was in use on North Second Street.

The *Bardstown Repository* recorded the following in September 1816:

> BIBLE SOCIETY, NOTICE TO THE CHRISTIAN PUBLIC. The friends of Bible societies are requested to meet at the Brick church in Bardstown on Friday the 20th of this instant, there is in many minds a desire to form an association then for the gratuitous distribution of the word of life. There will be a Sermon delivered at 12 o'clock on that day, and immediately after an attempt will be made to form a Bible society. This notice is one that all denominations of Christians are requested to regard. No party feelings can have place.

The Presbyterians met here until they erected a church in 1827. The Methodists then used the building until their church was built on East Arch Street in the 1830s. The Baptists also met here until their church was built in 1830. Right before the Civil War, the African Americans of the community met and worshiped there. They have continued to use the building and today the First Baptist Church holds the land title of Mr. Jones's church.

There were Methodist settlers and congregations in the county as early as 1785, but few were noted as living in town. Ferguson's Chapel Methodist Church, 6 miles east of town, was built in 1791.

On one of his travels, Bishop Francis Asbury of the Methodist Church visited Bardstown on September 16, 1814 as recorded in his journal. But it would be 1821 when the first Methodist preacher, Reverend Barnabas McHenry, was assigned to Bardstown. Within a year, his health broke and he discontinued active ministry. In 1825, Reverend Hubbard H. Kavanaugh was assigned here and organized the Methodist Church at Bardstown. He was noted on July 21, 1832 as the Methodist Episcopal minister giving a sermon on temperance at the Baptist Meeting House on North Second (Union Church). By 1836, Kavanaugh was reported speaking at the "new Methodist Church," which was located on Lot #58 on East Arch Street. This church was destroyed by the 1856 fire.

The second Baptist church in the state was Cedar Creek, about 3 miles west of town. It was organized and holding meetings by 1781. In Bardstown, the Baptists used the Union Church for meetings until they built on Lot #50 on Third Street in 1829. Samuel Carpenter and Henry Gore were trustees who held the deed to this lot. Carpenter, a lawyer and professed Baptist preacher, was preaching the sentiments of Barton Stone and Alexander Campbell in 1830 to the distress of the Salem Association of Baptists. The association sent directives to the churches to prohibit anyone who held the doctrines of Campbell, or called themselves reformers or New Lights, to speak in the church. The Bardstown church majority voted not to shut their doors to these speakers and this divided the congregation. Division was happening all over Kentucky, with the result that the Disciples of Christ were forming, leaving their congregations, and building churches. In Bardstown, the New Lights or reformers outnumbered the staunch Baptists and gained control of the meeting house in 1834.

Though the reform movement continued in Kentucky, in Bardstown it cooled, and Samuel Carpenter deeded the meeting house back to the Baptists in 1846. The Christian church movement met in homes and rented halls after this. Carpenter died in Bardstown in 1857.

This is the original Mill Creek Baptist Church where a split in the congregation in the 1830s created the Botland Christian Church about 1 mile away. This log and frame building was used until a new brick church was built in 1952.

Near the turn of the century in 1891, the Baptist Meeting House was destroyed a second time by fire on this site. They then determined to build on a different lot. The Disciples wanted to buy the lot, but the Baptists refused to sell it to them. It was sold to a Mr and Mrs. W.C. Lyon for $900. They turned around and sold it to the Disciples for $500. On May 9, 1894, the cornerstone was laid for the Christian Church in Bardstown.

In 1808, Bishop John Carroll of Baltimore created four new Catholic dioceses in the United States: New York, Philadelphia, Boston, and Bardstown. The diocese of Bardstown included the area now in the states of Minnesota, Michigan, Wisconsin, Illinois, Indiana, Ohio, Kentucky, and Tennessee. From this area would come 30 dioceses. The French native Reverend Benedict Joseph Flaget was chosen to be the first Bishop of Bardstown. After first resisting the appointment, he was consecrated by Archbishop Carroll on November 4, 1810 in Baltimore. Lacking funds to pay for his trip until a purse was collected from his friends at Baltimore, he was not able to travel to his diocese until six months later. "The boat on which we descended the Ohio became the cradle of the seminary and of the church of Kentucky." Traveling down the Ohio River by flatboat with his fellow priests, he landed at Louisville on June 4 and rode by wagon to Bardstown, arriving on June 9. Flaget wrote a letter in 1811, noting that there were 150 families in Bardstown, but only three were Catholic. He continued south to the Holy Cross area where he remained until returning to settle at St. Thomas outside of Bardstown in 1812.

After becoming acquainted with the Kentucky Catholics, Flaget began to plan the erection of a cathedral. Father John David wrote the following in 1811:

Bishop Flaget built Saint Thomas Church 4 miles south of town on the Thomas Howard Plantation in 1816. Also at that site was Saint Thomas Seminary and the rustic birthplace, in 1812, of the Sisters of Charity of Nazareth.

The Bardstown Christian Church was built in 1893 on the lot previously occupied by the Baptist church. After suffering two fires on this lot, the Baptists determined to build elsewhere.

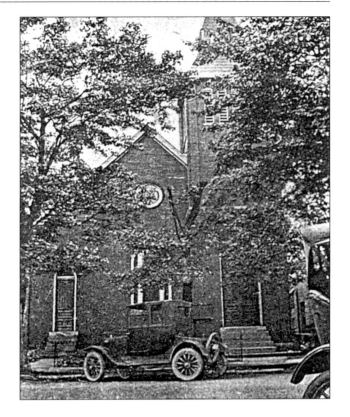

you are smiling, perhaps at the name of a cathedral of Kentucky, it is a matter of nothing less than a full-sized church . . . what will surprise you still more is the fact that the Protestants want it as much as the Catholics, they said that if we wanted to build a good, large substantial church, they would contribute generously.

As Bishop Flaget traveled around his diocese celebrating Mass, he passed around subscription lists. The statement:

> We the subscribers, do hereby obligate ourselves, our heirs, etc. to pay the sums, in cash or produce, annexed to our respective names for the purpose of building, in or near Bardstown, A Roman Catholic Cathedral Church, which will be large and handsome.

was followed by signatures of donors. Labor, materials, and money were promised to be called for in the future. A farmer gave $20 in "halling," a brickmaker $100 in bricks, a hatter $50 in hats, a blacksmith $25 in work, and an attorney gave $100 in services, which were used years later to sue for those promises that did not come forth.

This photo shows the plaster moldings and capitols that John Rogers formed and applied to the interior columns in Saint Joseph Cathedral.

Bishop Flaget had asked architect Maximillian Godefroy of Baltimore to provide him with plans for a cathedral, but when these did not materialize, he turned to John Rogers, a student architect of Godefroy who had recently arrived in Bardstown, for help. Rogers would design and supervise the construction of the cathedral, as well as many other buildings in the community.

On July 16, 1816, with great ceremony, the cornerstone of Saint Joseph Cathedral was laid and blessed by Bishop Flaget and seminarians. It is a limestone block placed on the top row of the foundation stones on the southeast corner of the main front. Already, bricks were being molded, stacked, and fired, over and over, to produce the estimated 1 million needed for the structure. The forests around the town provided large poplar trees, which were shaped for the interior columns. This wood was also used for most of the framing, flooring, and shingles on the roof. Dealing with volunteer labor and limited funding, the architect-builder Rogers found the pace slow to coordinate materials and workmen. After financial highs and lows, the building was consecrated with great ceremony on

August 8, 1819. The front porch, bell tower, and steeple were not completed until 1825, after additional funds were raised.

In 1803, the town trustees determined to provide a market house. This structure would serve for farmers and others to bring their fresh produce, meat, and other products to town for sale. However, a controversy broke out over where to locate it. After three months of discussion, a town vote for location resulted in a 41-40 vote for its erection on the west side of Arch Street where it intersects with Third, rather than in the public square. John Weller built the 45-foot by 18-foot structure and became the first market master. The cost of $120 was collected from an anticipated town tax of $150. The county provided the scales and guaranteed their weight. The town trustees employed a market master to assign space and oversee operations. Market Day was every Wednesday and Saturday. At this time, there were seven retail stores and thirteen taverns in the county. In 1810, the population of the town had grown to 821. Several years later in 1841, a contract was accepted to build a new two-story market house one block north on west Broadway and Third at a cost of $746.

The board of trustees made and enforced the laws, collecting fines when needed. They also assessed and collected taxes. They determined the ownership of lots, right-of-ways of streets and alleys, and supplied what security measures they could against fire, crime, and public nuisances. Some of the stipulations during this time prohibited everything from boiling "pates, pelts or other materials for the purpose of making glues," to not feeding oxen or horses in the streets. Other prohibitions were against grazing cattle or horses in any graveyard; removing any plank or brick from a grave; racing horses in the streets; shooting bullets at marks on city streets; killing a dog, cat, hog, or sheep and leaving the same in town for 12 hours; shooting a dog running loose on the streets; and blocking an alley or street for 24 hours. Several of these carried stiff fines, including "anyone who sells merchandise on Sunday shall be fined $2."

In May 1827, the city trustees appointed 12 persons to patrol—six from twilight until 1 a.m., six from 1 a.m. to daylight. They were paid 75¢ per night. These were probably the first paid policemen.

In 1805, the cry of "Fire!!!" rang out in the early morning hours. The large frame house occupied by Alexander McCown as a tavern (Lot #38) was totally consumed, with all the furniture, as well as the kitchen and house opposite the tavern occupied by Mr. Nixon. It appeared to have been intentionally set, since it broke out in a room that had not been used in several weeks. The townspeople were complimented for the rescue of neighboring property. McCown's loss was estimated to been about $5,000. The next day, generous townspeople contributed to a fund for his loss. One month later, *The Western American* printed this statement:

> Citizens of Bardstown, awake from your lethargy! This is not the first time you have seen the property of your neighbor consumed without being able to give the necessary assistance. Not an engine or fire hook

belongs to this place. This omission must be attributed solely to negligence. It is sincerely to be hoped that a Fire company will be formed without delay, as the surest means of protecting your property.

The board of trustees had already recognized the need and had authorized the purchase in 1804 of two ladders 30 feet long and two ladders 15 feet long with fire hooks. They required that citizens keep two full barrels of water beside their house and business at all times. Why these ladders were not in use in the spring of 1805 is a mystery.

In 1810, a tax of 35¢ per $100 was levied to purchase a fire engine at a cost of $850. During drought conditions, patrols were organized to watch for fires. Constant vigilance against fire in the wooden buildings and craft shops saved many structures, but in the fall of 1816, Rizer and Weller's gunshop was destroyed by fire. Nevertheless, they were soon able to rebuild and reopen for business.

In 1828, a local gentleman published his concerns that the new metal roofs now replacing the old wood shingles would attract lightning and be a fire hazard, not a fire preventive. The trustees determined to buy a fire engine for $300 in 1830. They had solicited funds from Saint Joseph College the year before and now were able to order the engine. After appointing James M. Wright as captain of the fire company, they also required every homeowner to buy one fire bucket and, six months later, to buy one more. Residents were to place the initials of their name on the two buckets. The penalty for failure to do this was $1, or $5 for each week. (These buckets were of leather.) Where to store the fire engine was answered by the building of an engine house in 1832.

The firemen were complimented on their performance on March 4, 1836 when, at about 4:00 in the afternoon, R.S. Webb's Carriage Shop (Lot #81) on West Market burned. With diligent effort, the firemen were able to save the two frame houses next to the shop. As the carriage shop was not fully insured, between $300 and $400 was raised to help defray the cost.

Each year, as equipment wore out and more equipment was needed, the trustees were approached for funds. In December 1839, the city board agreed to the making of three fire ladders for the use and benefit of the citizens of Bardstown.

In the War of 1812, Kentucky supplied militia and volunteers to the tune of four out of every six eligible men in the state to fight with the Army of the Northwest in Ohio and Michigan and in the New Orleans campaign. Their term of enlistment was three months, but several signed on for six months. They were at the tragic battle at the River Raisin and with Andrew Jackson at New Orleans. The Kentucky troops were always fighting in campaigns, not in garrison duty, and suffered more deaths in battle than soldiers of all the other states combined.

Of the 2,500 Kentuckians who arrived in New Orleans on January 4, 1815, only about 1,200 had weapons. Four days later, 1,000 of these, led by General John Adair, would hold the center of the line where the main attack by the British occurred. They gave a good account of Kentucky shooting. Known as sharpshooters, many a young man had sharpened his eye by shooting squirrels and other varmints for the bounty paid by the state in the late 1700s. Most of the duty was on land, but the United States fleet on Lake Erie chose 120 Kentucky sharpshooters to fire from the rigging of American ships to demoralize sailors on the British ships. The Bardstown men who went to war are not on a single list, but must be surmised from later sources. Dr. Burr Harrison was noted as being the inspector general of Kentucky troops with Major James Smiley as his deputy. Major Christian Hahn, Daniel Talbott, Hendley Talbott, Benson White, Charles A. Wickliffe, Alexander Moore, Richard Rudd, Martin H. Wickliff, and David Weller are other local names that appear on the lists.

After the war, several newspaper articles announced meetings of the veterans to receive pay and reimbursement for "lost horses" from their officers. There were also articles criticizing those men who didn't serve in this war.

Jacob Rizer's gunsmith work was noted as being of the finest. He worked his entire career in Bardstown (1806–1859) at a shop and residence on the northwest corner of Fourth and Arch Streets. Local soldiers of the War of 1812 may have carried his guns as they went to New Orleans to fight with Andrew Jackson.

On the Thomas Speed estate, just outside of Bardstown on the Bloomfield Pike, music could be heard coming from the old log house in the fall of 1818.

Charles Anderson Wickliffe, attorney and member of the Bardstown Bar, served during the War of 1812, as well as in the Kentucky legislature, the United States Congress, and as lieutenant governor and governor of Kentucky.

Anthony Philip Heinrich lived and composed in this log cabin. The immigrant from Prague played the violin in Lexington in 1818 and, later in the year, he lived in the log cabin on the Speed estate. "How Sleep the Brave" was composed to commemorate the heroes who fell at Tippecanoe and River Raisin in the War of 1812. He left the cabin by January 1819 and went to live at Farmington in Jefferson County. He left Kentucky in 1823 and eventually ended up in New York City where he held many successful concerts and music festivals.

During the War of 1812, William Bard, son of the Bardstown agent, was a revenue agent for the federal government and was required to collect the taxes placed on everything from "Pig iron to segars." He had the difficult duty of collecting from the distillers of the area. An additional tax of 20¢ had been placed on distilled spirits to help pay war debts. In a long article in the *Bardstown Repository*, he warned the distiller that a violation of the law is viewed by the collector as a disgrace to any man and a bad example to the community at large.

In 1811, 2,000 distillers were listed in Kentucky, mostly small farmer- or miller-owned operations. Recognition of the "art and mystery" of the craft of distilling

Adam Anthony purchased a building in 1809 for 3,000 gallons of whiskey. He traded promissory notes for whiskey paid him for stills to Richard Stephens for the east of lot #76. At the same time, he paid $1,700 for the west of the same lot, "where Anthony now lives," pictured above.

was given at the agricultural fairs of the state as whiskey makers competed against each other. This spread the fame and enhanced the sale of the product outside the local areas. James Cox, local distiller in 1814, advertised, "I have for sale about 40 barrels of excellent whiskey."

At this time, Bardstown coppersmiths Lewis Quigley, Ebenezer Bard, Daniel Wehrley, and Adam Anthony were making and selling stills of every size. They received copper from Baltimore and advertised that they would take whiskey in trade. Anthony purchased a building in 1809 for 3,000 gallons of whiskey. He traded promissory notes for whiskey paid him for stills to Richard Stephens for the east of lot #76. At the same time, he paid $1,700 for the west of the same lot, "where Anthony now lives."

Local sales were made in jugs, but shipping the filled oak barrels down the rivers to the southern markets was thought to have aged and mellowed the whiskey. In 1820, a mortgage was recorded by John Black, John Crozier, Peter W. Grayson, N. Wickliffe, W.P. Duval, and Ben Chapeze on "all the stock of goods including whiskey now on their boat." These shipments by flatboat to Natchez and New Orleans started in the 1780s and continued until the late 1850s. The first steamboat arrived at Louisville in 1811, but shipping by flatboat remained the main way to send agricultural products to the south for several years. Flatboats were loaded and waited for the winter floods to float down the rivers to the Ohio. In later years, they were unloaded on to steamboats at the mouth of the rivers.

In 1805, a listing of arrivals at Natchez mentioned boats from Bullitt County carrying lime, from Salt River with whiskey and cider, Salt River with cider and potatoes, Salt River with potatoes and apples, Clarksville with beef and pork, and a Barge from Cumberland with horses. Some merchants would advertise that they would take whiskey in trade to be sold to the southern markets. In the summer of 1819, Peter Wickham advertised that he had merino wool and whiskey for sale. The wool was priced at 75¢ per pound and the whiskey was noted to be 80 to 90 barrels of first-rate new and old whiskey. This old whiskey was probably less than four years of age.

The ability to navigate the Beech Fork became a political issue in the 1819 election, when Charles Wickliffe and John Hays printed their positions on improving the Beech Fork River with locks, "a scheme proposed for improving the Navigation of the Beech Fork." Hays stated the following:

> This is a project which would awaken the prosperity of Bardstown and diffuse life and vigor into the surrounding county. It would raise the price of Town property, increase the value of Land all over the county, open a rich channel for commercial enterprise and bring home a ready market for his produce to the very door of the Farmer.

It was a politician's pipe dream to dredge and straighten the narrow, shallow, and winding river—it didn't happen.

On April 4, 1852, the newspaper reported, "a steamboat came within 12 miles of Bardstown a few days ago and discharged freight," the only recorded boat coming up the river.

The Bardstown Bar was known far and wide. In fact, one of the most famous of local lawyers moved here to practice after he heard that Bardstown lawyers could demand higher fees. Ben Hardin was practicing law in Hardin County in 1812 when he went to the jail to offer his services to a prisoner. A Mr. Bray had been drinking with his friends when one of them became sick and his stomach "brought forth its contents." Bray was curious and put a candle to the contents to determine if it was whiskey. In the ensuing fire, the man burned to death and Bray was arrested for murder. Bray asked Hardin how much the fee would be. Hardin told him $400. Bray's answer was, "For $400 I can get a Bardstown lawyer." Hardin went home and told his wife to pack up; they were moving to Bardstown. The final outcome of the story—Hardin successfully defended Bray, Hardin got the $400 fee, and Bray got his Bardstown lawyer.

The Pleiades Club was the name given to the illustrious group of Nelson County lawyers of this time in Bardstown. Charles A. Wickliffe, Ben Hardin, John Hays, Ben Chapeze, Felix Grundy, and William Pope DuVal made up the six members of the debating club. John Rowan and John Pope also participated in the debating activities, though not of the original six. All but one would go on to national recognition.

According to Ben Johnson, Felix Grundy was the most capable of the group. He was elected to the Kentucky legislature at 22 years of age. He became a judge of the court of appeals, later chief justice and founder of the circuit court system. He moved to Nashville, became a Congressman, and then was the Attorney General of the United States from 1838 to 1840.

Ben Hardin was the most popular. He studied law at Bardstown under Grundy. He served several times in the Kentucky Senate and lower House and was Secretary of State under Governor Owsley. He was elected to the House of Representatives in Washington, serving more than ten years.

Charles Wickliffe served as an officer at the Battle of Thames during the War of 1812. He served in the Kentucky legislature, the United States Congress, and as lieutenant governor and governor of Kentucky. From 1841 to 1845, he served as postmaster general in President Tyler's term. On August 1, 1844, Wickliffe was the object of an assassination attempt while on board the steamboat *Georgia*, on her trip from Old Point Comfort, Virginia to Baltimore. Charles A. Wickliffe was stabbed twice in the breast by J. McLean Gardner with a clasp knife. Gardner was found to be insane and sent to an asylum.

William Pope Duval was made the subject of three of Washington Irvines's *Crayon Papers*. After serving in the War of 1812, he returned to Bardstown to practice law and was elected to Congress. In 1822, he was appointed the territorial governor of Florida where he was reappointed twice, serving until 1834.

John Rowan was elected and served in the Kentucky House of Representatives for 15 years. He was appointed Secretary of State in 1804 under Governor

All the buildings in this view of East Market Street were built before 1830 except the courthouse. Unfortunately, only four of them remain in 2000. The others removed are, from the left on Lot #93, the brick home; on Lot #92, the two-story frame building in front of the Chapeze House; and on the right, the last two buildings at the end on Lot #77.

Christopher Greenup. He was also a United States Senator from 1825 to 1831 and later held the office of judge of the court of appeals. He also served as the first president of the Kentucky Historical Society from 1838 until his death in 1843.

John Pope served in the Kentucky legislature, as Secretary of State from 1816 to 1819, and as the congressman from Kentucky for five years, then was appointed governor of the territory of Arkansas from 1829 to 1835. Afterward, in 1835, he returned to Kentucky and the office of congressman.

Ben Chapeze was a highly respected lawyer in whose office were trained many young men.

But of all these distinguished men, the one who was considered the greatest orator was John Hays. He, but for his weakness for drink, might have surpassed the others in greatness. However, while intoxicated, he met his untimely death at a thief's hands.

Other lawyers of the time were Richard Rudd, T.P. Linthicum, W.M. Roberts, Will L. Thompson, and William Jeff Merrifield.

Slavery was an institution in Kentucky from the early years. Slaves were willed to family members, but many servants were emancipated when their owners died. Some were given the choice of going to Liberia, as part of the American Colonization movement, and others had to leave the state after being freed. In the 1820s, slaves couldn't inherit property unless they were freed, but how can freedom be purchased without the funds of the inheritance?

This coin silver chalice and paten was presented to Reverend Patrick Kenrick by his Bardstown friends before he left to go to Philadelphia as bishop in 1830. The gift was crafted by silversmith and monk Felix Cashot.

Austin Hubbard, prominent citizen of Bardstown, died in 1823 with no immediate family to inherit his property. His will devised all of his property to "Narcissa, a mulatto girl that I have raised," if her present master would let her go for a moderate price; if not, the estate was to go to a cousin. The court appointed Thomas Wathen the administrator, but the will was contested by Peter Sweets, who had purchased the cousin's interest for $100. The will was finally declared valid in 1831 after going through all the appeals. At that time, Narcissa was the property of William Elliot of New Haven. She was 25 years of age and had two small boys. Wathen and Sweets falsely told Elliot and Narcissa that there was barely enough money in the estate for Narcissa's freedom, but not any for the two children. They agreed to pay Elliot $350 for her manumission if she would sign a relinquishment of any further claims to Hubbard's estate. At this point, the true value of the estate was learned as Sweets sued Wathen for the remaining amount of about $3,000. Narcissa entered this suit with a cross-bill claiming fraud by Wathen and Sweets in obtaining her relinquishment of her claim.

When Narcissa died in 1835, she left a will, leaving her estate in trust to John McIsaac and Nathaniel Wickliffe for the benefit of her two minor children. The trustees continued the suit in an appeals court. In the decision in 1842, Narcissa's claim of fraud by Wathen and Sweet was affirmed, and the remainder of the estate awarded to the trustees. McIsaac and Wickliffe then reached an agreement with Elliot that the children, then ages 16 and 18, would be freed when the oldest reached 21. One man's legacy freed three people.

Taverns and hotels were buildings of renown where travelers and local folk met, ate, and exchanged news. Deals were made and depositions were signed on the same tables where three meals a day were served. In Bardstown in the early part of the century, many taverns operated. They changed hands frequently, but the tavern building continued to function as a hotel, restaurant, and saloon.

It was announced in *The Western American* in June 1804, "Wm. R. Hynes just received from Baltimore and is now opening at his new Store House fronting on the public Square a large and general assortment of merchandise." This was the stone building on the southwest corner of the public square. Hynes, the first owner, resided there in 1812. In 1830, he rented the tavern house and contents to Thomas R. Elder, who operated it as the Bardstown Hotel until 1832. In 1833, Simeon B. Chapman rented the house and lot, formerly occupied as a tavern by Elder. Hynes sold the household furnishings to Chapman as part of the lease. The listing of these included 42 Windsor chairs, 10 single beds and underbeds, 15 low-post bedsteads and cords, 6 dining tables, and many other items, indicating the capacity to sleep at least 25 people and seat more than 40 at the tavern. Chapman advertised the Bardstown Hotel in 1833, at the sign of the Golden Eagle. He held tavern bonds from 1833 to 1838.

Richard Head operated a tavern on the northeast corner of Fourth and Market from 1802 until his death in 1825. His son-in-law Charles Holloway and his widow Ruth ran the Head & Holloway tavern at this same site. In 1827, they printed scrip to use in their tavern, which they gave as change. This was a common practice among merchants as silver change was scarce. By 1833, Michael Rentch was innkeeper at the same building under the sign of General George Washington. Before joining his mother-in-law, Charles Holloway had operated a tavern on the northeast corner of the public square in the Brashear house in 1826, known as Washington Hall.

In June 1819, James Green announced that he had:

> opened a house of entertainment in Bardstown in the White House on Cross Street running by the Court House and formerly occupied by a tavern, where he enlarged his buildings and rendered them much more comfortable, as well as his stables. His table will at all times be well furnished as the county will afford, his bar supplied with the best of liquor and his stable with everything requisite as well as active attentive ostlers, also a few genteel borders when can find their own lodging, would be taken.

This was the Columbian Inn, operated by Green, where Bardstown friends of Reverend Patrick Kenrick presented him with a silver chalice and paten before he left Bardstown to go to Philadelphia as bishop in 1830. The gift was crafted by silversmith and monk Felix Cashot. This building was the tavern run by Joshua Wilson in the 1790s, James Crutcher, from 1802 to 1805, then Micajah Roach and later his widow Ruth Roach until 1818. It was a two-story log structure that may have been erected as early as 1786. A boarding and coffee house was operated by Madison Miller in 1833 at this building. The Great Bardstown Fire of 1856 began at this tavern in a trash-filled backyard.

In the *Bardstown Herald* on January 5, 1831, William Penny informed the public that he would run a tavern, Lafayette Hotel. It was to be located on the corner of Third and Arch, being the house where the Centre Bank was formerly located, and would include the genteel dwelling of Moses Black next door, as well as a new building he was constructing. There were two new stables. Traveling dentists rented rooms for dental surgery; "C.M. Way has taken a room at the Lafayette Hotel where he proposes to practice dental surgery." Six months later, dentist William Cross from New Orleans was also at Mr. Penny's hotel. He remained in town for a few days. He placed teeth, both real and artificial, from a single one to an entire set. He also extracted, cleaned, filed, and plugged them. In 1832, Powell and Bard took over the Lafayette Hotel, where "Mr. Penny is the Louisville and Lebanon Mail Carrier and leaves from here."

Education was always sought for the youth of the community. Salem Academy, first designated the Bairdstown Academy, was established prior to 1785. Dr. James Priestly was the best known of the many teachers there during the 40 years of operation. It was supported by local subscription and educated many young men, who became leaders in their field in Kentucky. The location of the original building is unknown, but the second building is clearly documented. The September 8, 1807 *Candid Review* notes the following:

> the building for the use of the Salem Academy being now completed, on Thurs. 10th instant the Trustees of the said Academy intend delivering possession thereof, to Mr. McAlister, the President. On that day an appropriate oration will be delivered by one of the trustees. The citizens of Bardstown and its vicinity are requested generally to attend precisely at 10 o'clock at the Court House to walk in procession to the Academy. By order of the Board, Thomas Speed Sec. All who subscribed for the building of academy at Bardstown will find their subscription in my hand, John Weller.

This new structure was located on land donated by Walter Beall on the northeast corner of the town preemption, near the present intersection of North Second Street and the railroad.

In 1815, it was announced that Stephen Chenault and James McAllister would oversee the Salem Academy seminary. The terms of tuition were reading, writing, and arithmetic at $15 per annum, or English grammar; geography, with the use of the globes; Latin, Greek, and French; algebra and mathematics; and Natural Philosophy or such sciences as are usually studied in public seminaries at quarterly payments of $30 per annum. "The public may rely on the assiduity and zeal of the tutors in instructing their pupils as effectively and extensively as their own acquirement and the opportunities of the institution will admit." This is the last reference to the school as Salem Academy until 1837 when F.X. McAtee is noted as operating the school.

In 1816, Bardstown Academy was advertised as "again open for the reception of pupils under the supervision of Mr. John Proctor." The trustees were John Rowan, Thomas Speed, and Burr Harrison. (They were former trustees of Salem Academy.) It is surmised that this school was held at the same building and was still in existence in 1819.

Another reference which may refer to this building was in 1831: "Reverend Spencer Clark will open a school in the vicinity of Bardstown at the old seminary on the first of April next. Where all branches necessary to the acquirement of a classical education will be taught."

The Sisters of Charity opened Bethlehem Academy in 1819. Reverend John David, the founder of the Sisters of Charity, purchased the brick house of Nehemiah Webb for $800. It was located on outlot #8 on South Fifth Street. In the early years, only three nuns staffed the day school and its enrollment was

The Sisters of Charity opened Bethlehem Academy in 1819 in the brick house purchased for $800 of Nehemiah Webb. They operated a school here until it was rented to the McAtee sisters in 1837 for an English School. Later, Bethlehem Academy was reopened by the Sisters of Charity.

small. The nuns lived at Saint Joseph College with the sisters, who were helping at the seminary and college. On August 8, 1836, *The Catholic Advocate* recorded, "Joseph Hazeltine advertised for sale or lease, the house and lot near home of Hon. B. Hardin in the vicinity of Bardstown known by the name Bethlehem School." Hazeltine was a manager for the college and later for the Sisters of Charity at Nazareth. It appears that the small enrollment determined the closing of the school. In December 1837, the Misses C.L. and Mae McAtee announced that they would operate an English School in the house recently occupied by Sisters of Charity in the southwest section of Bardstown.

In the 1830s, new private schools seemed to pop up every year. In an advertisement of December 1830, John A.Y. Humphrey, local school teacher, proposed to conduct a night school at his schoolroom from the hours of 6 p.m. until 9 p.m. for the purpose of giving lessons in reading, spelling, and various forms of penmanship. The terms were to be moderate and accommodating. The candles necessary were to be furnished by each subscriber. This opportunity to attend school at night was unusual and useful to the many apprenticed workmen and other adults who earned their living during the day. The subscription list of December 1830 for the 90-day quarter showed 19 pupils, each paying $3 a quarter for instruction in English grammar and geography with map use and

This is the front door of Bardstown Female Academy, a private school for girls operated by the Presbyterians. Architect John Rogers designed this building for James M. Browne as a residence c. 1820. It had a curving stairway to the third floor with beautifully carved woodwork.

construction, and $2.50 for instruction in reading, writing, and arithmetic. Many subscribers paid in merchandise from their businesses as one gentlemen withdrew his son from school and asked for the bedstead returned which he had credited the teacher. Humphrey also operated Bardstown Old Academy in 1834, noting there would be four weeks of vacation in the summer.

A newspaper advertisement noted the following:

> Bardstown High School will open in Bardstown on Jan. 23, 1833 with Messrs. Gazlay & Taylor. To be taught on the Lancasterian or Monitorial plan of instruction. It will be taught in the upper room of the brick building adjoining Michael Rentch's Tavern [on the northeast corner of Fourth and Market Streets].

The "Monitorial" method used older students to instruct the younger ones.

The Presbyterian-published newspaper *The Western Protestant* announced the following in the fall of 1837:

> The Trustees of the Bardstown Female Academy has purchased the residence of Colonel James M. Brown on the Louisville road—1/2 mile from the Ct. House and will have it ready for boarders and pupils by December 1. Will be able to accommodate 100 boarders. Reverend Nathan L. Rice has been appointed Principal of the school. Trustees, D.S. Howell, C.A. Wickliffe, Joseph Brown, Charles Nourse, Jacob Rizer, John McMeekin, Wm. Sutherland, James M. Browne, H.H. Hopkins.

Architect John Rogers designed this building for James M. Browne as a residence *c.* 1820. It had a curving stairway to the third floor with beautifully carved woodwork. The private school for girls was operated by the Presbyterians. S.S. McRoberts succeeded Rice as president in 1839, with several special instructors such as "Julius A. DeLaBarthe [from Paris] Prof. Of French, Spanish, languages at the Bardstown Female Academy [who] will give private lessons in these languages and also to conduct a school of fencing."

The *Bardstown Herald* newspaper, in January 1831, presented a choice of new educational opportunities: "John Farmer proposed to open a school in Bardstown," or "The Classical & Mathematical Seminary has opened in the Wickliffe's brick building—board $27.50, etc."

If one attended a school without music or dancing, private lessons were available in 1837 at the "Advanced Dancing School—Monsieur Mallet from New York a Professor of Dancing opens Dancing Academy at the Smiley House. $15.00 a quarter—30 lessons." The Smiley House was located on Lot #63 and was a boarding house. Or, in the spring of 1832, Mr. H.C. Welch and Schoolcraft informed the ladies and gentlemen of Bardstown that they had associated themselves for the purpose of opening a music school.

But the most ambitious undertaking was Saint Joseph College. In the Fall of 1819, newly ordained Bishop John David moved the major seminary of Saint Joseph into the unfinished brick structure next to Saint Joseph Cathedral. Writing to his friend Father Simon Brute, he said, "I have taken them (the 3 priests and 12 seminarians) here to form a clergy at the cathedral and to help in teaching at the college we have just established, a little against our inclination, but to satisfy the public who expected it."

Bishop Flaget had been approached by parents of young boys who wanted him to open a school of Christian education. In the basement of this building, the first classes of Saint Joseph College were held. Flaget turned over the college responsibility to the recently ordained Reverend George A.M. Elder with the guidance of Bishop David, who had charge of the seminary. It was a day school at first, serving young men of the town and nearby areas, but the desire of parents for a "sound English education" with discipline and form was reflected by the growing number of applications for new students. The first enrollments in 1820 were 30 students with the number doubling to 60 in a year. In February 1822, a proposal was made to take in boarders. Less than five months later, letters reflect that boarders were being received. The 1822 prospectus noted that 100 students could be accommodated with no more than 30 boarders, and that tuition would be $40 for the higher branches, $28 for the common branch. Boarding and tuition, including wash and mending, was $125.

One year later, in June 1823, the report noted, "100 students 25-30 of which are boarders." This steady growth necessitated new buildings. President Elder and Joseph Hazeltine, college procurator, were directed to consult with the merchants of the town as to their feelings about the expansion and funding of the new buildings. Their favorable report encouraged the contracting of architect John Rogers and the borrowing of money for the additional college buildings.

The first structure built specifically for the school was a two-story brick building, which had an open porch on each level used as a hallway or passage. Constructed in 1822, it was followed two years later with another brick building of three floors, which was directly to the north and parallel to the first one. But they still needed room. A new building was designed. In a June 9, 1825 letter, Bishop David wrote the following:

> Our building is advancing very rapidly. It is I believe 120 feet long by 40 wide, with two wings which are already built. The one on the south side, which is the old college, is at least 60 feet long; the other is more than a hundred, comprising the kitchen with its compartments, the meat house, the laundry; and above many rooms for the sewing of the Sisters and to iron the clothes, with a piazza to make it dry in winter, etc. The north wing contains on the ground floor a refectory, the room of the economist, or agent, on the first floor, the physics laboratory, the room of the professor, and study hall, on the second floor, the wardrobe and the infirmary. The attic, in V-shaped roof makes a large dormitory. The

Saint Joseph College was built in three stages in 1822, 1824, and 1826. Two parallel buildings were joined by a large front wing to create the college building known as Spalding Hall.

large new building will contain on the third floor and in the attic, some dormitories; on the second, rooms for the professors; and on the first, writing rooms, drawing rooms, music rooms, etc. Underneath are some vast cellars, well lighted, which will serve for various purposes that I do not know as yet.

Incorporated by the state of Kentucky in 1824, the college was empowered to issue BA and MA degrees, the earliest recorded in 1827.

In the spring of 1825, Father Bertrand Martial brought "56 students—boarders from New Orleans and the neighboring territories, all Catholics." The front wing was not completed and these students crowded the facilities.

Three months later, Bishop David reported on the building, which was to be finished in a week, and also that "Our college is well organized and is doing fine. We have in all 90 boarders. That is as many as we can lodge for the present. . . . The number of externs at the college is about 100." The externs were those students who lived in town or with their parents and attended school. Their tuition was reduced, but they were expected to adhere to all the rules of the college.

In 1828, the following was written, "Fr. Martial is back and is determined to remain among us. He will be able to do a great deal of good at the College,

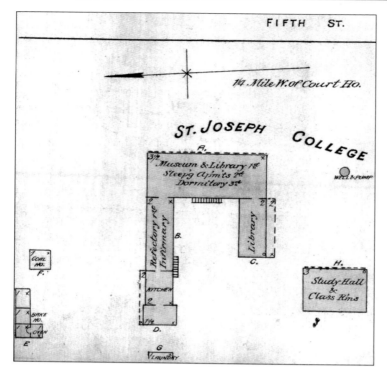

This 1879 map shows the shape and use of the main building of St. Jospeh College. The 1837 fire began in the large front section, which was gutted by the blaze.

composed in a great part of Creoles, who have a great deal of confidence in him." Flaget continued to have faculty changes. On June 6, 1830, college professor Reverend Francis Patrick Kenrick was consecrated bishop of Philadelphia by Flaget. (He was the fourth bishop to be consecrated by Flaget and would later become the sixth archbishop of Baltimore.)

The Reverend Martin J. Spalding was appointed professor at the college and pastor of the cathedral in 1835. He would bring about the creation of a college magazine and a Catholic newspaper, which continued for 13 years. He returned from Rome at the request of Flaget to help in the college.

In the spring of 1836, George Penny's accommodation stage, fondly known as "Old Long Tail Blue," brought confusing reports about the Texas-Mexican conflict in the mail bags. Newspapers printed every rumor. Local interest was high because of the young men who had left the Bardstown area to go to Texas.

The Kentucky Mustangs, a volunteer militia group made up of recruits from Kentucky, included Captain Burr Harrison Duval and his 19-year-old brother John Crittenden Duval; Richard Brashear; William Jefferson Merrifield; John Donohoo; William Mason; and possibly two more from Nelson County. The Duvals were sons of William Pope Duval, the first territorial governor of Florida, who lived in Bardstown before his appointment and continued to own a residence there at this time. They had attended Saint Joseph College in the early 1830s. The men were in the group of about 400 others surrendered by Colonel James Fannin and massacred at Goliad, Texas on March 27.

In the group of Mexican officers at the same battle was a Lieutenant A. Martinez, who won honors for English rhetoric at Saint Joseph in 1832 and had been a roommate and particular friend of Brashear. They shared reminiscences of old times during the week of the Americans' captivity. Duval said that the last time they saw their Mexican friend, on the morning of Palm Sunday, he had "an apparent affectionate smile on his countenance and walked off laughing." John C. Duval was one of the very few who escaped the massacre and wandered for weeks before reaching civilization to report the details. His first-hand report was published in the *Bardstown Herald* in May of 1836. Duval remained in Texas and wrote a history, *Early Times in Texas.* He was known as "the first Texas man of Letters" and died in 1897, reportedly the last survivor of Goliad. He was very critical of Martinez. Another Kentuckian, Benjamin Franklin Hughes, who was spared at the massacre but was sent as a prisoner to Matamora, reported that, cruelly mistreated and beaten by soldiers, he might not have survived except for the kindness of Martinez. Maybe Martinez was trying to make up for not being able to save his classmates from death at Goliad. There was much speculation and conversation by those at the college who remembered these young men.

One of the most upsetting events in the college history occurred on January 25, 1837 when fire destroyed the interior of the front section of the building. A heavy odor of smoke had been noticed for some time before fire was discovered in the roof sheeting. It had come from crevices in the chimney and spread under the roofing. Furniture was pitched from the upper-floor windows in a vain attempt to save it from the flames. The only things that survived this treatment were the feather beds.

There was no hope to fight the fire because of the height, but diligent efforts were made to save the two parallel buildings. *The Catholic Advocate* noted that college officials reported that they would immediately proceed to have the front "refitted" and had no doubt that, in a few months, they would be able to occupy it again. The total loss was reported to be $25,000, with insurance of only $10,000. They expressed their hope to have it ready by the next September. The school was rearranged to accommodate the students and classes in strained conditions, but it continued operation.

The greatest loss of the fire took place eight months later in September when beloved President George Elder succumbed after the exertions during the fire damaged his heart. Ben Webb noted that "the tolling of the cathedral bell announced his death after two weeks of suffering." A procession of sorrowing friends more than a half-mile long followed his body to the Nazareth cemetery.

Reverend Martin John Spalding was appointed president of the college on October 1. He was faced with completing the restoration of the main building, raising the funds to pay for it, and fulfilling all the duties of the president while serving as the pastor of the cathedral. In late July of 1838, Spalding was presented with a resolution from the City Fathers. They were outraged about an invasion of young men on a previous Sunday evening, singing vulgar and obscene songs, and displaying loud and disorderly conduct. The "quiet citizens of this town" did not appreciate these activities. The resolution condemned the actions, admitted they could not identify the culprits individually, but all agreed it was "the college boys."

Spalding mourned in September 1838 that only one-eighth of the students were Catholic. During this time, there was great confusion over accounts, lost letters, and many students leaving the school. He issued directives to local merchants not to open accounts with students of Saint Joseph College without proper authority.

Newspapers are a great source for historical research, but at this time in Bardstown's history, there were a limited number of newspapers printed. The first pages of these were filled with national and statewide news. The desire to know the national happenings was understandable as the local news was spread by word-of-mouth. Local ads and news columns were located on the back page. The first recorded paper printed in Bardstown was *The Western American*, published by Francis Peniston in 1803, who moved to Louisville in 1806.

The *Candid Review* followed, published by Peter Isler from 1807 to 1811. Other papers with names similar to this were the *Impartial Review* in1806, *Candid Critic* in 1807, and the *Candid News* in 1808. It is not clear if these papers were the same as the *Candid Review*, as no copies are found preserved. A notice in the *Kentucky Gazette* on May 7, 1811 indicates that a "newspaper is about to be published at Bardstown, *The Herald of '76* by Shadrach Penn." There is no other reference to this paper in the early records and if it was published, it was probably only for a short time.

The *Bardstown Repository* was published by different owners from 1811 until about 1821. *The Western Herald* was issued between 1824 and 1830, followed by the *Bardstown Herald* from 1830 to 1837. Two papers began life on the same day in February 1836, *The Catholic Advocate* (1836–1841) and *The Western Protestant* (1836–1838). *The Protestant & Herald* (1838–1842) and the *Kentucky Mirror* (1837–1838) complete the papers printed until the 1840s. The pre–Civil War period was reported by the second *Bardstown Herald*, which was printed from 1850 to 1855, as was the *Bardstown Visitor* (1849–1856). The *Bardstown Gazette* was printed off and on from 1841 to 1860. Of all these papers, less than 20 percent of the published copies survive for research. Microfilm of the archived papers has been reviewed for much of this historical account.

In 1828, *The Western Herald* office was east of the courthouse in the McLean building. D.D. Jones, the printer, advertised that he had received new job type from Cincinnati and would print invitation cards, magistrates blanks, sheriffs blanks, hand bill, ball tickets, etc. Also in the McLean building on February 13, 1836, the first issue of *The Catholic Advocate* weekly newspaper was published. The editors were Reverend M.J. Spalding, Reverend George Elder, Reverend Hippolyte de Luynes, and Reverend William Clark. It was an eight-page weekly, printed by Ben Webb and M. Fletcher. A subscription was $3.50 a year. (They also had 25,000 Russia Quills for sale at the printing office.) "Our object is not attack, but defense." This was a response to strong crusading against the Roman Catholic

Church, with written and verbal attacks by Protestant ministers such as Presbyterian Reverend Nathan L. Rice, who would publish *The Western Protestant* in the same year. One month later, the Webb and M. Fletcher partnership was dissolved, with Webb continuing to run a print shop. In September, it moved to Arch Street next door to Mr. McMeekin and McLean's store. It continued at Bardstown until 1841, then relocated to Louisville, still under Ben Webb and Spalding. It ceased operation on July 21, 1849.

On June 10, 1837, there was the notification that a new "weekly literary, political and commercial paper *The Adventure* will be published by James D. Nourse and B.J. Webb." Research hasn't uncovered if this paper was ever printed.

Theatrics, horse racing, cock fighting, dancing, barbecues, and getting your profile cut for framing were all occasions for entertainment in the early nineteenth century. In the 1807 *Candid Review*, the following was written, "Profiles taken with physiognotrace, by Lewis Hocber at Dr. Harrison's Stone House in Bairdstown. The profile painted in water colors and they can be furnished with gilt, black, and plain frames. He does description of sign painting on moderate terms." In Bardstown in 1807, the students of the Salem Academy exhibited at early candlelight the celebrated farce, called "The Mocking Doctor."

The military units of the county, such as the Bardstown Rifle Company (1809) and the First Brigade (1815), drilled and marched in parades for Fourth of July and other patriotic occasions.

In this three-story building on the southeast corner of the court square, known as the McLean House, two newspapers were printed. The Western Herald *was printed by D.D. Jones in the 1820s and* The Catholic Advocate *was printed by B.J. Webb in 1836. The building was used for a short while as a post office and as offices for doctors and lawyers.*

In the fall of 1816, you had a choice of entertainment: the Bardstown Races commenced on October 30 and ran for four days, or you could attend the Cotillion Party given by Patrick Jones at Mr. Roberts Ballroom, held on October 1 and every other weekend. In the 1820s and 1830s, you had a choice of live animals or amateur theatrics. "A Grand Menageries—Living Animals—Elephant, Lion, Shetland Pony" was to be exhibited at J. Roberts's on September 2 and September 3, 1828. Admission after 4 p.m. was 25¢ and children under 12 got in for half price. In 1831, Elder's Tavern Ballroom showed the celebrated comedy "The Rivals," "presented by 'The Bardstown Thespian Corps.' " Admission was 50¢ for adults and was similarly half price for children under 12.

But the events anticipated by all, most especially by politicians, were the barbecues at Sweets Bath Spring. "In commemoration of American Independence Day, Michael Sweets will prepare a public barbecue dinner on July 4, near the Cool-Bath Spring, where all those ladies and gentlemen is expected to attend. A separate arbor will be prepared for the ladies. Dinner will be ready at 12 o'clock precisely." The bath spring was a rock-walled, spring-fed pool directly over the hill from east Beall Street. Many orators filled the shaded grounds with rousing political and patriotic speeches. A stage with scenery and props was erected for outdoor performances at the bath spring. In 1838, John R. Frisley & Company would give a "theatrical performance" at the spring after paying for a $5 license.

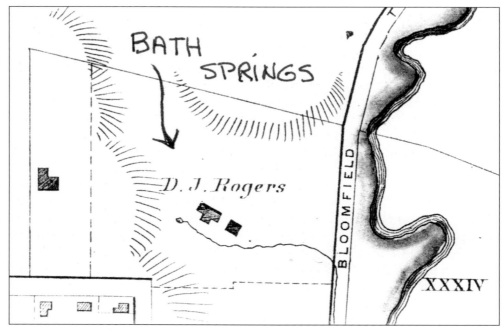

An 1882 map still shows buildings at the Bath Spring. The cool, water-fed basin and the heavy woods provided relief for hot-weather meetings. It was reached by the Bloomfield Turnpike. The spring fed into Town Creek, which is the dark line to the right.

In *Collins History*, the annals noted on July 31, 1837 that Richard Clayton, a Cincinnati aeronaut, floated over Nelson County from the direction of Louisville. He descended for dinner (noon meal) 7 miles north of Bardstown and afterward ascended and floated high enough for views of Bardstown, Shepherdsville, Fairfield, Taylorsville, and Bloomfield. He again descended at 7 p.m. on Cox's Creek 5 miles north of Bardstown after having traveled 100 miles.

Horse racing in Kentucky arrived when a fellow rode a horse over the Cumberland Gap and met another on horseback in a field of bluegrass. The first Bardstown newspaper, *The Western American*, ran this advertisement on November 2, 1804: "Bardstown Races!!! On the second Friday in November a subscription purse will be run for over the course in Bardstown, free for any horse mare or gelding that has never won a purse (three miles the heats)." On the subsequent days, the heats were shorter. They were using the Frankfort Jockey Club Rules. In September 1816, the announcement was made that the Bardstown Races would commence on October 10 and continue for four days. Those wishing to enter a horse were to apply to Martin H. Wickliffe three days in advance, or they would have to pay a double entry fee.

In the 1830s, a more organized group held these meets. Bardstown's Jockey Club was organized on September 18, 1838 with more than 100 members. Each paid the sum of $10 annually for a term of three years. The Honorable Ben Hardin was president of the club; T.P. Linthicum, secretary; Daniel S. Howell, first vice president; Colonel Ben Doom, second vice president; William Heavenhill, third vice president; and F.G. Murphy, fourth vice president. John S. Daniels, James M. Doom, John Murphy, E.H. Hinton, J. Wood Wilson, J. Dedman, and Ben Wight were elected stewards. A ladies' committee was organized with D.S. Slaughter, John McMakin, John Rowan Jr., Thomas P. Crozier, G.C. Slaughter, J.S. Wilson, and William Doom.

The race course was a 1-mile tract and was located east of the Louisville road between the railroad extension to Springfield and the land purchased for a public cemetery in 1856. Many horses from Kentucky and Ohio, famous in their day, raced for the purses over this track. The first race was held on October 24, 1838 and continued throughout the week. Eight horses were entered for the first race— 1 mile and repeat. The second day, the race was for 2 miles and repeat; the third day, 3-mile heats. The second meeting was at J.N. Eastham's hotel on September 14, 1839, with new officers elected and arrangements made for the upcoming races beginning October 8. All horses raised in Nelson County were admitted free. The purses were $50 for 1-mile runs, $200 for 2 miles and repeat, $300 for 3-mile heats, and $400 for 4-mile heats. A purse of $150 was given for the best three in 5-mile heats. The third meeting was held at the Lafayette House on March 14, 1840. At the spring races, which began May 26, 1840, the meeting was dull. The secretary reported the following:

> The track was very heavy there having been a continual rain of several
> days previous to the commencement of the races. The attendance was

small and consequently very little amusement as well as betting, was going on. The extreme badness of the track will account for the slow running. The soil on which the track is made of a clayey nature and the racing on it the day previous had worked it up so that the mud had become nearly as tough as whit leather; so that a horse under speed would sink under nearly up to his knees's every jump.

In August of 1840, the secretary was ordered to prepare a synopsis of the races and have it published in the *Lexington Intelligencer*, *Louisville Journal*, and *Bardstown Gazette*. John Hunter, William Maden, Benjamin McAtee, Wilson Bowman, and Felix Murphy were appointed to rent out booths and put the track in good condition for the coming races. The leading horse owners who entered the races were L.Y. Drane, L. Davenport, A.L. Beauchamp, George Able, W. Bowman, G. Goffeen, and F.G. Murphy. The latter owned a sorry-looking mare named Motto, which was a winner in all the races in which she was entered. The records of the club continue until 1843 and it is supposed that the Bardstown Jockey Club was discontinued.

The old buffalo trails that had been improved for horse and wagon travel, and the creek beds that served as wagon roads, were to be abandoned for the new "Macadamized" stone-based turnpikes. In the 1830s, turnpikes were being constructed by companies funded by local shareholders. These companies contracted the building and operation of the roads. Toll keepers at toll houses located about every 5 miles, starting 1 mile from the town, collected the charges for the use of the "pike" and turned these amounts into the turnpike companies. In 1836, the Bardstown and Louisville turnpike was controlled 10 miles from Louisville by the Louisville Turnpike Company, with the balance by the Bardstown Louisville Turnpike Company. At the same time, the Bardstown and Springfield turnpike was ready to let-to-contract. The shareholders in the Bardstown Green River Turnpike Company met at the tavern house of Abraham Smith in 1837. These improved roads provided a much easier surface for stagecoach travel. "George Penny's Stage leaves from Chapmans's Hotel 3 days a week—fare $3 goes to the Galt House in Louisville." A second stage line set out to compete with George Penny.

Travel to Louisville from Bardstown on the stagecoach involved catching the coach at "Mr Elders in Bardstown at sunrise" on Sunday, Tuesday, or Thursday, and arriving in Louisville late in the afternoon. An accommodation line of coaches, operated by S.T. Beal and Company, left Bardstown every morning and arrived in Louisville the same day. The stagecoach left Louisville the alternate dates, leaving at sunrise each day, passing through Mount Washington, and by Nazareth if desired. Passage was $2.50. Gentlemen with families constituted four passengers and were charged $9. Passengers met at Throckmorton's Inn in Louisville and Mr. Elder's at Bardstown.

3. Before, During, and After the Civil War, 1840–1870

This community declined in importance in state affairs, leadership in education, and religion. It was not growing economically. The pre-Civil War tensions and apprehensions cumulated in the division of the town when the call of the Confederacy was answered by many young men. The greatest test was the occupancy of the town by the Union authorities for more than four years. After the war soldiers returned, but things were never going to be the same.

A visitor to the town during the 1840s and 1850s could still stay at the taverns or hotels that travelers had used 20 years before. They were under different ownership or operation, but many remained in the same buildings. In 1840, Ludwell Able was noted as the tavern keeper at the Hynes House. In 1845, Michael Donohoo purchased the building known as the Hynes House from the heirs. The *Bardstown Gazette* reported a social occasion there in June 1855. It was advertised that "if weather rainy—carriages will be available to and from the party." At this hotel in October of 1859, a "Prof. Block optician, featuring Brazilian Pebble Spectacles for nearsighted" rented a room for four days to serve the public. In 1865, Donohoo sold Hynes House to Reverend George W. Robertson, who renamed it Shady Bower.

Another hotel was constructed in 1842 by Julius de la Barthe on Lot #49. It was known as the Mansion House. In 1856, the hotel was operated by George W. Moore and J.T. O'Bryan as a hotel and stage stand. In the same year, J.T. O'Bryan and John C. Talbott were proprietors of the Bardstown Hotel, the same building with a new name. In 1859, Talbott was shot and killed by an intoxicated patron of the saloon. His wife Amy continued to operate the Bardstown Hotel in partnership with J.T. O'Bryan, with her son Daniel Talbott Jr. as agent. Later in the century, this would be known as the Central Hotel.

As reported in the *Bardstown Herald*, in court on April 14, 1852, "County Judge Stone refused to grant any license for the retail of ardent spirits. There were a number of applicants. The course of the Judge is warmly approved by about nine-tenths of the community." What effect this had on the taverns of the community is not known. The Sons of Temperance Nelson Division #48 met every Saturday night at their hall on the corner of Main and Arch Streets. Officers elected in June 1855 were John H. McQuown, W.M. Powell, T.A. Jones, W.H. Wetherton, A.E

Mason, G.W. Jenkins, R. St. Clair, Alfred D. Hynes, James Queen, and A. Milburn. There was a Temperance Party in Kentucky at this time, which offered candidates for governor and lieutenant governor.

It became apparent to the Bardstown trustees c. 1840 that the graveyard on south Fourth Street was running out of space. The trustees set up committees each year after 1840 and finally bought some land from Dant south of the town. Immediately, they decided it didn't suit and began to try to buy land from Doom and Hart on the Bardstown-Louisville Turnpike. In November 1852, the trustees agreed to purchase 7 acres from Doom and Hart at $120 per acre. Dr. Hart agreed to take the lot purchased of Dant at cost. The December survey and plat shows 13 acres. An agreement was made with the Saint Joseph congregation to take the north half, and Bardstown to take the south half, with the passage to be between the two properties. It was divided equally after the right-of-passage was taken out. The trustees portion constituted 6 acres, 3 rods, and 8 poles at $816. In the spring, the trustees authorized the grading and fencing of the graveyard. In 1859, lots were marked and fencing surrounded the cemetery. Burials were already occurring in the "new graveyard."

Traveling entertainers between 1840 and 1870 still provided a variety of excitement for the community, but sometimes fun was as close as the nearest bath house. The trustees permitted Bryan C. Oneal to do the following:

> to erect a Bath House in the Eastern end of Main Street and below the public spring so far as not to injure the same . . . privilege granted for 10 years as long as it is kept in good repair, etc. Also right is granted for Oneal to use rooms in his said Bath House for public balls or dances.

In the 1850s, the entertainment included an exhibit of pictures of Adam and Eve, Swiss Bell Ringers, and a professor of mesmerism. You could also entertain yourself with having your image made at "Webster & Holland, daguerrean artists," or at "N.M. Booth bookstore, selling music and stationary with a Daguerrean room." In 1859, Professor R.A. Boyd, the blind pianist, violinist, and vocalist, was to give a concert. The license fee was waived.

In December 1856, the celebrated Germania Troupe arrived and consented to entertain at Mattingly's Hall. Some amusements in 1856 were more for the men. "Cock Fighting has become a favorite amusement here. The feathers fly most awfully." You could also bet on racing, "a foot race came off in this vicinity, on Thanksgiving Day, between a brag runner from Louisville and a young man of this neighborhood, distance fifty yards. Our young man beat the Louisvillian three feet."

A September 1858 art exhibit of "Photographic Art at Mattingly's Hall" was announced to last but one week longer, "exhibited at the Louisville Fair." Two years later, on October 6, 1860, E.W. Pierce opened a "Gallery of Art" in the boarding house of Ben C. Watts, where he executed all styles of pictures. In 1860, Busch's Sax-Horn Band offered to play at "Fairs, Barbecues and political meetings. Moderate prices—Wm. Busch leader."

Doctor Alfred Hynes was a true Unionist. In his house on the court square in Bardstown, he not only treated the sick, he recruited troops for the Federal army. Dr. Hynes had one son serving the North and another the South.

After the Civil War, visiting performers returned to town in May 1865. W.V. McCann was licensed to perform ventriloquism, and the Curry, Storm, and Ginger Minstrels performed after paying a $3 license.

The Bardstown trustees were responsible for safety, sanitation, and law and order in the town. The trustees directed that all the horse racks on Third Street between the courthouse and the market house, as well as all horse racks on Arch Street, be removed, as they were declared to be a nuisance. They also directed that the cellar doors of the Shadburne property, then occupied by John E. Sweets on Third Street and the McMeekin property on Flaget, be declared nuisances and be fixed within 10 days. The Bardstown trustees continued to work for the safety of the town by buying fire equipment and building cisterns for firefighting water.

In the 1840s, there were numerous references in the city minutes to cisterns built or repaired, only to be used for fire protection. A fine was imposed if water was taken from them without permission. Most were 10 feet deep and 10 feet in diameter. They were located at major street intersections and filled with the run-off from the buildings.

In July 1841, the appointed committee met to draw up rules for the Bardstown Fire Company. It was not to have more than 30 members. The fire company in 1841 consisted of thirty members, one captain, and three lieutenants. They exercised twice a month in the months between April and October, and once a

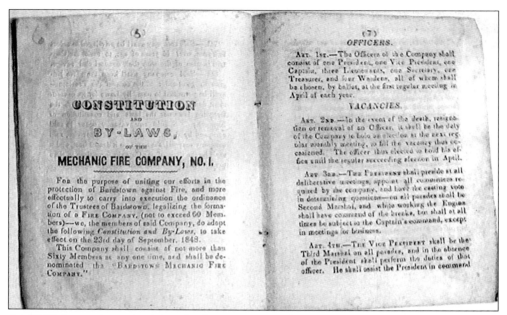

In 1847, it was determined that the fire company could be enlarged to 60 members and a new company organized. This 14-page Constitution and Bylaws of the Mechanic Fire Company, No. 1 was published by W.W. Jack in Bardstown in 1849.

month the other months. They kept the engine in good repair. To provide protection for the engine, a fire house was built in the spring of 1842 at a cost of $235. Complaints about fire hazards in old log buildings, or stables and cracked chimneys in buildings, were brought to the trustees' attention. They directed that the buildings be emptied or taken down and the chimneys repaired.

It was an honor to be accepted in the fire company. Its members were leaders in the community, and it functioned as a public service and social group. In the 1850s, committees were formed to purchase a bell for the fire engine house, to contract for the painting of the engine and market houses, and for someone to keep the engine and make repairs as necessary.

In May 1855, Independent Fire Company No. 1 was organized. J.C. Wickliffe, John E. Newman, J. Darwin Elliott, Edward M. Haydon, G.G. Schaub, Charles Clusker, John Simmers, Nathaniel Crough, O. McDonald, and Horation Nicholson were elected officers.

Their talents were called for when fire broke out on April 12, 1856. Trash that had accumulated in the Ten Pin Alley behind the Old Columbian Inn on East Market Street ignited and quickly engulfed the old wooden tavern building. The strong winds from the southwest pushed the flames north and east across Market Street and up Second Street. Houses along Second and almost to the bluff on Arch Street were consumed. Twenty dwellings, the Methodist church, and other buildings burned. Forklore has it that the firemen were getting ready to dynamite the Presbyterian church to make a fire break when a rain storm came up and drowned the fire. Boys from the college were commended for their help at this time. Every able-bodied man fought to keep the flames from devouring the town. For a few years afterward, the area was referred to as the "Burnt District."

In 1858, the trustees appropriated $300 for a new engine house. The building plan was drawn on the original minute book with the description of details. The engine building was to be 30 feet wide, 45 feet long, 14 feet high with a hip roof, 2 front panel doors, 8 feet wide and 10 feet high, with a side door 4 feet wide and 10 feet high. The house was to have four windows and one back door, 12 feet wide and 10 feet high. The walls would be of brick and the whole building was built of good material with "properly painted" woodwork. The old engine house was sold at public sale to the highest bidder. It was removed and the new one was built on the old site at the intersection of Broadway and north Third Street, directly across from the market house. The area around the engine house was paved. In the same year, Bardstown borrowed a fire engine from the Louisville Fire Department while theirs was being repaired.

The new engine house was complete and in use by late 1859. A review of costs in February 1860 noted that the total cost was $1,086.58. The amount of money raised was only $514. This included the sale of the old house for $35.10; donation from Saint Joseph College of $50; the Variety Club donation of $125; M. Jupin's donation of $4; and the trustees' appropriation of $300. This left a balance of $572.58 still owed. The records do not note how it was paid off, but the engine house was used for more than 60 years.

Paying off a new engine house wasn't the only expense in the next few years. The yearly cost of a messenger for the fire company was about $120 and, in 1861, it was paid to Francis Smith. In 1863, William Sisco reported to the board that the hose belonging to said engine was very defective by "reason of burst." The probable cost of 1,000 feet of suitable gum hose for the fire company, with or without brass joints to the different sections, wasn't estimated, but a year later, 500 feet of hose was ordered at a cost of $813.15. The city also paid the fire company $120 for taking care of the engine for a year. They sold the old engine for $50 (hopefully, they had replaced it with another). James Malona was appointed to have the fire hooks of the town repaired or new ones made as, in his opinion, it was necessary. They were also directed to look into the cost of the hook-and-ladder carriage. James Malona and E.E. Green were appointed to purchase such material as was necessary for the construction of the carriage and cause the same to be constructed. The bids for such a carriage put in by Sisco and Poynter were rejected. In 1869, James Malona was paid $6.55 for a fifth wheel for the hook-and-ladder wagon, plus $3.20 for traveling to Louisville to buy 600 feet of hose.

While the city fathers were managing the town's problems, another human drama was unfolding in a house on Third Street. This was the story of "Anna, the woman who bought her husband twice."

In the 1830s, in Bardstown, lived Felix Cashot and Peter Gates, two former Trappist lay brothers who were watchmakers and silversmiths. They had remained in Bardstown since 1809 when the first settlement group of monks returned to Europe. They lived and worked in a brick house on Lot #49, two blocks north of the courthouse on Third Street. They rented rooms, made coin silver, and repaired clocks and watches. Cashot was the dominant one of the pair, making the business decisions and contacts. Their housekeeper Anna was a mulatto slave about 33 years of age in 1839. She was acknowledged as the principal blue dyer of the community and also sold linsey and janes, materials that she had woven. A blue-dyer was one who was experienced in using indigo dye to color woven cloth or yarns. Anna was "an intelligent woman, honest in her dealings."

In the spring of 1839, Anna came to Felix Cashot with a problem. Her husband Nick was the servant of John Ricks, a farmer in the Cox's Creek area. Mr. Ricks had suffered some financial difficulties and was forced to sell his slaves "down the river." If Nick was sent "down the river" to New Orleans or to Natchez, Anna feared she would never see him again.

For many years, Anna had worked and saved her money to purchase Nick's freedom. She had been assured of her freedom by will at Cashot's death. Cashot allowed her to do work for others after she had finished her household duties. By this time, she had saved more than $300, but she needed about $350 more. Cashot agreed to loan the money to her with Nick hiring out to repay this debt. Cashot purchased Nick from Ricks and Nick then moved into the Cashot household. He worked for various men about town and paid on the loan. Everything appeared to be working out for the couple, but the sudden death of Cashot in August of 1839 brought complications to this arrangement.

Cashot's will, written in 1833, mentions the names of the slaves he wished to emancipate, but Nick's name was not one of them as he wasn't owned by Cashot at the writing of the will. The executor of the will, Peter Gates, was left most of the estate. He was called by some "a dull man," who "retired as much as he could from interaction with the world." He was influenced by Julius de la Barthe, an immigrant from France in 1838, who boarded at Cashot's while teaching French and dancing in the community. De la Barthe claimed to be ignorant of business practices, but he ended up owning all the real estate left to Gates by Cashot. Nick was retained as part of the estate and hired out. Anna was now free, and she continued to spin, weave, dye, and sew, earning and saving money to again purchase Nick's freedom.

By 1845, Anna succeeded in purchasing and freeing Nick, but she felt she had unfairly paid for her husband twice. She determined to sue to get her money back from the second purchase. Anna was respected and supported in this effort by the community. Charles A. Wickliffe, former governor, acted as her attorney. Jonathan Rogers, cabinet maker and neighbor of Cashot, testified to Anna's honest and industrious nature. John D. Nicholson, owner of the Broadway Mills, a cotton spinning mill, testified to her business dealings and the fact that she was allowed to keep the money she earned. She had done blue-dying for him. Christian Kuhl, a music instructor at Saint Joseph College, lived at Cashot's after the college building burned in the fire of 1837.

He gave a deposition about Nick's freedom to go out to earn money for the repaying of the loan.

The case came to court in 1845. Anna wanted the money refunded that she had paid the estate for Nick. The weakness of the case was the absence of any written record concerning the loan of money or the amount of money Anna contributed to the purchase by Cashot. After the depositions were read and the testimony was heard, the jury found that Nick owed the estate only what money was borrowed from Cashot, deducting the amount already earned by his labors before Cashot's death. The jury thought he should have been freed after this amount was paid by his labors between 1839 and 1845, when Anna purchased him. Anna was awarded $600 by the court as a refund of the second purchase.

The estate appealed this judgment to the Kentucky Court of Appeals. In the final action reversing the decree, in 1849, the court of appeals ruled that Anna's money earned when she was a servant of Felix Cashot belonged to her master. Therefore, all the money spent in 1839 to purchase Nick belonged to Felix Cashot and there would be no refund of the money spent to re-purchase him. In fact, she now owed Gates $600!

Anna Cashot and Nick Ricks continued to live in Bardstown at the intersection of Broadway and north Fifth Street. At Anna's death in 1857, her heirs, a brother and a niece in Marion County, sold the house to Saint Joseph College. Records indicate that Nick was still around after the Civil War, but the couple appeared to have had no children. Anna would have certainly been an inspiration to any

Anna Cashot's case was argued in the stone courthouse on the left, depositions of the witnesses were taken in the Hynes House in the center, and her case was filed at the circuit clerk's office next door. The building on the right was the Brashear House, later called Lawyers' Row because of the many attorneys' offices there.

descendants because of her character and loyalty to her husband. She worked and saved for more than 15 years to set him free.

Up to this period, all the schools were private or subscription schools. The Kentucky legislature in 1838 passed a school law that required counties to lay out school districts and create both county and district school governance, but it failed to require the county courts to impose taxes to pay for the operation of the schools.

In February of 1852, Phil C. Slaughter, commissioner of common schools of Nelson County, announced the election to choose three trustees for a common school being organized in town upon the district system. All widows having children were entitled to vote with the free male inhabitants of the district. In July, the Bardstown district elected school trustees. The trustees of Bardstown set up a board to ascertain the number of children ages 6 to 18, find a place to hold school, and find suitable teachers of English and the dead languages. They were to set salary and determine what subscribers could be obtained from the public. In April 1853, Samuel Carpenter appointed an agent to procure a suitable person to teach school and to do all other acts of a school agent. The board of trustees of Bardstown were to establish and maintain a common school or schools adequate to the teaching of all children within the corporation of Bardstown. However, a year later, the School Tax was voted down by a vote of 78 to 55 in the Bardstown election.

This is an 1859 view of the Bardstown Female Institute (1844–1908) when it was operated by the Methodist Episcopal Church South. In 1864, it was incorporated as a stock company with trustees as the Baptist Female College.

The Bardstown Female Institute opened in 1844. Four years later, it was advertised for sale. The ad noted that Bardstown had a population of 2,000 people. In 1854, it was under the "patronage of the Louisville conference" of the Methodist Episcopal Church South. In 1855, the graduation of Mr. Morrison's Female Institute was held at the Methodist church. In 1864, the school incorporated as a stock company with trustees as the Baptist Female College at Bardstown.

In 1849, Dr. Jouett Vernon Cosby changed the Bardstown Female Academy to Roseland Academy and ran the school until its suspension in 1895. In the fall of 1858, the city trustees gave permission for them to build a stable on their property next to Beall Street.

On March 10, 1853, Saint Thomas Orphanage had just opened and had about 55 boys. Saint Joseph College was prospering under new leadership. In the fall of 1848, the Jesuits took over the operation of the college with the blessing of Bishop Flaget. The first official announcement about the transfer of the school to the Jesuits was made on July 20, by President Edward McMahon. At this time, there was still $23,000 in debts. It was announced that Father Peter J. Verhaegen, now president of Saint Louis University, would take over the college. The following was reported:

> On July 24, 1848, six members of the Society (S.J.) left St. Louis on the steamboat "Ocean Wave" to take possession of St. Joseph's College, Bardstown. After stopping in Louisville for an audience with Bishop Flaget, they continued their journey and arrived by stagecoach at Bardstown on Friday afternoon.

After inspecting the building and premises, it was determined that a $2,000 loan would be needed to fund the necessary repairs. It was obtained from E. Baker Smith, a Catholic resident at Bardstown and former trustee of the college. Immediately, they began the repairs. College opened with 60 boarders and 40 externs in September 1848 at a newly repaired and refurbished campus with a new faculty. The students' dining room, kitchen dormitories, and infirmary were the responsibility of the Sisters of Loretto for the next four years. The first commencement of Saint Joseph as a Jesuit institution was held on July 18, 1849, when eight graduates received Bachelor of Arts degrees.

It was observed that the number of non-Catholic students increased at the school. It was thought to be the result of southern Protestant families sending their daughters to Nazareth Academy, 3 miles away, and their sons to Saint Joseph. The Catholic students always outnumbered the Protestant by at least two to one.

The Jesuits continued the celebrations on Washington's Birthday and Saint Patrick and Saint Joseph days. An account of the 1849 Washington Birthday affair included the following: "Amid the cheering notes of 'Yankee Doodle' we retired to the refectory where an excellent dinner was prepared by the worthy President and Faculty." Many toasts followed. One toast was noted: "to the students of St.

Joseph's 'E Pluribus Unum'—though many in number, may they ever be one in mind and heart." At a similar celebration in 1854, inscriptions of praise of Washington in the languages of English, Hebrew, Greek, Latin, French, Spanish, Italian, Flemish, and Dutch were hung on the entertainment hall walls.

The college population slowly increased as word spread of the Jesuits' success. In the summer, Walter Hill, prefect of studies, and another professor would accompany students home to the south and recruit others as they traveled. This was a practical move, as steamboat travel had improved to the point where the trip south could be made in five days. Meeting up with returning students, they accompanied them back to Bardstown and the fall term of college.

The rattling of sabers echoed throughout the south in the early months of 1861. Since so many of the students of Saint Joseph College and Nazareth were from the southern states, which were seceding, uncertainty and confusion filled the students in both schools. The Jesuits determined to hold the commencement exercises two weeks early on June 21, so southern students could return home before military lines were tightened. This was the last commencement in the history of Saint Joseph College under the Society of Jesus. One Masters degree and seven Bachelor degrees were awarded. The registration of this school year was 280, only 14 of which came from the northern states.

The Jesuits tried to open the college classes in September of 1861, but the registration was only 38 boarders and 29 day students. Of these, only eight boarders were received during this tense time. Henry Lawler was the next-to-last student registered at Bardstown. In September 1861, he "took his trunk and walked off, reported that the college had broken up on account of the War."

The Jesuits planned to send the boys home or to transfer them to the school in St. Louis. There were problems in getting them through the southern lines, so the youngest of them, including several Mexicans, went to St. Louis. By early December, only reduced faculty remained at the school.

Tensions before and during the Civil War were felt by the local authorities. The trustees dealt with law and order enforcement in an inconsistent hiring, firing, and laying off of police. In March 1854, the trustees dispensed with the police until further notice. During the occupation by the Union during the Civil War, the trustees appointed different numbers of patrol at different rates. Most of the time, the provost marshall had troops patrolling the town, but in September 1863, four men were appointed city watch for six months at $20 per month. Marshall Davis Auld reported that the citizens had subscribed $60 to help pay for the police watch. This was to give them 5 percent more than the board had approved.

After the war, in 1865, Police Judge John Marnell was also the market house master, who had the authority of keeping the scales and renting the stalls, and Thomas O'Neal was elected marshall, with three policemen. Six months later, a police force of six men was appointed to be selected by the chairman of the trustees. Later, the policemen were paid $25 a month.

In 1860, the Bardstown & Louisville Railroad arrived in town. Stocks in the corporation had been sold and its completion was eagerly awaited since the project

A brick wall was constructed in the front of the Saint Joseph College campus in 1852. The two lodges at the front were for the porter, who checked students in and out, and a tailor. The tailor met with the students to fit them with new clothing and repair their old garments. The wall was torn down in the 1920s.

had begun in 1856. The arrival opened up travel of goods and people to and from Louisville and communities along the way. A published train schedule indicated one could catch the morning train at Bardstown at 7 a.m. and arrive at Louisville at 10:20 a.m. To return the same day, one would board the train at 2:15 p.m. and arrive at Bardstown at 5:08 p.m. If a person boarded in Louisville, the times were reversed. The railroad arrived in Bardstown just in time for the Civil War.

In the spring of 1861, the war drums were beating throughout the South. Kentucky was holding to a middle line of no involvement. Political maneuvering kept the state government from committing to support for her southern sisters. This stance of neutrality gave the southern sympathizers a sense of security from Union control or invasion of the state. Behind the scenes, the Unionists were plotting to set up recruitment camps and shipping arms into the state to arm those recruits. The Confederates were also recruiting over the state line in Tennessee. As soon as the Union camps opened, the Confederates moved up into Bowling Green and accepted soldiers to the cause. Union camps of instruction were located throughout central Kentucky. These camps had a two-fold purpose: first to prepare the new soldiers for military life and battle, and second to occupy the state with troops. This method of intimidation continued for the next four years.

Nelson County was in the center of much of the controversy. First, the location of the turnpikes and the railroads dictated the movement of many troops and

The Kentucky legislature created the State Guard in May 1860, allowing volunteer militia units to be organized in each county. The Nelson Greys and Stone Riflemen were the Nelson County Units. This picture, taken at the first encampment at Louisville in August 1860, shows Governor Beriah Magoffin in the center.

supplies through the area. Turnpikes were stone-based roads capable of handling wagons and heavy travel in all types weather. Many families were split in their loyalties, fathers, sons, or brothers, husbands and wives. Soldiers from Nelson County fought for both sides during the conflict, but a larger number served the Confederacy than served the Union. The occupation of Bardstown by Union troops began in September of 1861 and ended in September of 1865. As one local woman later remarked, "I couldn't step out my kitchen door without stepping on a Yankee soldier."

In the spring of 1861, many Bardstown citizens were choosing sides in the coming conflict. Nancy Crow Johnson, wife of William Johnson, was on the committee of southern women who selected the flag design for the Confederate States of America. When she was telegraphed the final decision, she and her maid sewed the design into a flag, which was publicly raised in front of their home before an estimated 5,000 people.

Ex-governor Charles A. Wickliffe of Nelson County attended a secret meeting of Unionists in April at the Capitol Hotel in Frankfort. They planned to supply arms secretly to loyal Union forces at key points in Kentucky where there was a danger that the State Guard would take control for the Rebels. President Lincoln supplied 5,000 guns on May 18 to be parceled out to loyalists. On January 29, Wickliffe had been one of six commissioners to a peace conference in Washington, trying to keep Kentucky from seceding.

Meanwhile, officers and soldiers of the local Nelson Greys or "Home Guard" were arranging their affairs to go to war.

In September 1861, John Hunt Morgan arrived with his men at Camp Charity, 7 miles from Bardstown and 3 miles from Bloomfield. On Friday evening, September 20, knowing that the State Guard was about to be disarmed by the Federal authorities, Morgan, commander of the Lexington Rifles, had loaded the company's arms onto two wagons and started toward Lawrenceburg. Morgan and the rest of the company, who wanted to join the Confederacy, slipped away after dark, the next day riding toward Lawrenceburg and Bloomfield. They were joined by most of the Nelson Greys at a farm located on the Middle Branch of Simpson's Creek. Who arrived first, the Nelson Greys or the Lexington men, is not known, but the site was probably chosen by Captain John C. Wickliffe, leader of the Nelson Greys.

Bloomfield's sympathies lay with the South and could be counted on for support and recruits. It had been reported that the 10th Indiana Infantry was to move to Bardstown, so that location was not safe. The creek supplied water for men and horses. The community supplied food and other supplies without accepting payment, whence came the name "Camp Charity." Rebel-fed rumors of an attack on the Federal troops at Bardstown kept them on alert in their garrison. When Morgan and his recruits left on September 28, they were uncontested by the Federals as they made their way to Fort Albert Sidney Johnson at Bowling Green. The Nelson Greys were known as Company B of the 9th Kentucky Regiment and belonged to the 1st Kentucky Brigade, later known as the Orphan Brigade. Other recruits served with Morgan's cavalry.

Young William Carothers and Tom Porter of Bardstown set out to "go to war" and join the troops at Camp Charity near Bloomfield. The following passage is from Carothers's diary entries:

> Camp Charity near Bloomfield Ky. was a place where recruits for the Confederate Army were rendezvoused to go South with Colonel Crepps Wickliffe. Being anxious to join this army and my mother being opposed as she was a Union woman, I was forced to leave home without telling any of my family goodbye. A bright day, with my friend Tom Porter and our guns upon our shoulders, we passed down the street past the Court house and out Market Street. Dr. Harrison McCown called out to us "Where are you going boys?" "To the War" we gaily replied and we passed on. The news was reported at once to my mother and she was advised as I was but seventeen, to get out a warrant and have me arrested and brought home by legal authority. We were out three miles on the Bloomfield road when we were overtaken by the Sheriff Arch Thomas. The sheriff conducted me in triumph to my mother who affectionately

This picture of Company E of the 10th Kentucky Volunteer Infantry was taken three days after they mustered out in Louisville on December 6, 1864. The Union unit was organized in November 1861 at Lebanon, Kentucky.

told me that if I would wait until I was a few years older then it would be alright with her. My friend Tom went on and went out with his comrades on the march to Bowling Green. A stray shot killed him before he arrived in Bowling Green.

Meanwhile, Union forces, 10th Indiana Regiment, camped in the Bardstown area as early as September of 1861. They were soon followed by other units until about 11 were spread around the community. The Indiana officers contracted with Saint Joseph College in early November to furnish fresh bread for the soldiers, with them supplying the flour. The bake house and kitchen facilities were not being fully used at this time because of the closing of the school. Mattresses were also requested to aid the sick and given by the Fathers without request for payment. As the different troops arrived in the area from the northern states of Pennsylvania, Ohio, Indiana, Illinois, Michigan, Wisconsin, and Minnesota, as well as Kentucky, they brought sick soldiers who lived in close quarters spreading illness.

The Federal authorities approached Father Verdin to rent rooms and beds in the college for sick soldiers. On Christmas Day, the first patient was brought in and before long, half of the available space of the college buildings had been given up to sick and disabled soldiers. As many as 300 to 400 people, including attendants, filled the rooms formerly used for education and living quarters. Twelve ladies from the community were in constant attendance on the soldiers. Nine returned to their homes in the evening and three were provided lodging at the college. A number of Sisters of Charity also nursed at this hospital. One devout lady, Mrs. Hays, was remembered for her patience and spiritual example, which produced many baptisms among these backwoodsmen from Western states. Young men died from disease during this period at the hospital: meningitis, measles, inflammation of the brain, consumption, dysentery, all hazards of unsanitary camp conditions. The army doctors and local doctors were helpless to save them with the medicines of the time. All day long, large groups of convalescent soldiers and friends strolled along the hallways. Outside, the traffic of wagon trains bringing supplies or sick soldiers was a constant rumble. The Jesuits performed their ministry and noted that "of the soldiers, as many as one hundred and eight were baptized, a large number of them dying from wounds or disease."

There were at least two other buildings used as hospitals, the cotton spinning mill on south Fourth Street and the Female Academy on North Third. The local provost guards visited the hospitals each day. Their unpleasant duty was "burying the soldiers who die in the hospitals. There is about six hundred in the hospitals at this place and they die at the rate of about four per day." In 1867, these Union soldiers were removed from their first resting places and moved to the national cemetery at Lebanon.

Camp conditions were dismal as a letter from Absolom A. Harrison of Hardin County at Camp Morton, Boyles Regiment 4th Kentucky Cavalry explains:

> Our camp is four miles from Bardstown on the turnpike leading to New Haven. It was very nice in a woods pasture place when we first came

Written on the back of this picture is the notation, "Corporal Nicholas M. Wayman, 1st Ky. Vol. Cav. FF 16th 12, at Bardstown, August 1861, native of Marion County." He appears to be holding a powder flask and a sword.

here, but it is knee deep in mud now. I would like to be home but I got myself in this scrape and I will have to stand it. But if I live to get out of this, I will never be caught soldiering again that is certain. We don't get more than half enough to eat and our horses are not half fed and everything goes wrong.

The big Federal encampment south of Bardstown was on the land owned by William Sutherland, a wealthy farmer and distiller. On January 21, 1862, soldiers Samuel H. Calhoun and Beswick, both of the second Kentucky Regiment, killed a shoat belonging to Sutherland. Sutherland saw them and complained to the camp authorities, even though Calhoun threatened his life if he did so, a threat that Sutherland apparently did not take seriously. The two men were given a minor punishment, if any. On the morning of January 23, Calhoun went to Sutherland's house, finding him at breakfast, and told him that one of his soldiers had killed one of Sutherland's heifers and that he would show him where it was in a thicket. Sutherland finished his breakfast, then went unsuspectingly with Calhoun, who then shot and killed him.

There were tracks in the field from the place where Sutherland's body was found leading toward the camp. Charles W. Thomas, neighbor and a friend to the Sutherlands, was one of those who noticed and followed the tracks across a muddy wheat field. The principal investigator of the crime was Captain J.H. Green of the 35th Indiana. Suspicion fell on Calhoun and Beswick because of the incident of the pig.

Calhoun had made arrangements for another to answer for him at assembly and had slightly disguised himself on going to Sutherland's house, so that it was not

The State Guard encampment in Louisville in 1860 gives an idea of the look of the training camps around Bardstown in the winter of 1862.

easy for those who had seen him there to be sure about identifying him. His appearance and manner convinced many of his innocence, including the chaplain, but he told Beswick that he had killed Sutherland. While confined in the Nelson County jail, declaring his innocence, he wrote an incriminating note to a comrade, which was intercepted.

On January 28, a court martial was convened on which there were three colonels, four lieutenant colonels, three majors, and two captains, one of whom was Captain Green. There does not seem to be any record to that effect, but it would be a good guess that the court martial met in the courthouse. On January 29, the court cleared Beswick and convicted Calhoun of murder. Shortly after the conviction and sentence of death, Samuel H. Calhoun, the murderer of Mr. Sutherland, requested permission from Colonel William H. Lytle, the commandant of Camp Morton, for Captain J.H. Green to be allowed to write a story of his life. Colonel Lytle was quick to give his consent. For the next few days, Green and Calhoun must have spent all their waking hours together, Calhoun describing his life and Captain Green writing it all down. He confessed to more than 13 murders, starting when he was 14 years of age.

A letter of Bernard Reilly, soldier of the 7th Pennsylvania Cavalry, described the hanging:

> Yesterday we were ordered to march. At Bardstown, we joined the 35th Indiana, and a Michigan Regiment. The prisoner was brought out, and placed on his coffin, in a wagon. He did not seem to mind it. He laughed and talked as if he was not at all concerned in the affair. We marched 6 miles to Camp Morton, where the scaffold was erected, and from 10-15 thousand volunteers placed around. We being the escort, took up our position very near the scaffold. The prisoner mounted the scaffold, and viewed the large assembly with complacency. He made a short speech, and turning to where his regiment (2nd Kentucky) was, he said in a loud and firm voice, "Farewell Boys," at the same time waving his hat and smiling at them. He turned and examined the rope, trying whether the noose would slip right. He then asked for the cap which he leisurely placed over his head and then held his hands behind his back, to be tied. He then stepped on the drop, which fell immediately. He died very hard, kicking for about 2 minutes. I never saw such coolness.

The procession was led by the 35th Indiana, then the 11th Michigan, 24th Kentucky, 1st and 2nd Kentucky, 7th Pennsylvania cavalry, and the 4th Kentucky Cavalry. Eight regiments of infantry and two of cavalry on the parade ground of the 22nd Brigade, approximately "8000 men," watched Calhoun hang at 2 p.m.

Absolom A. Harrison's company was acting as provost guards in Bardstown, living in a vacant lot. "We also have to put out patrols of 5 or 6 men to walk around town and arrest every soldier without a pass or drunken men and put them in jail until they can get sober." A military pass was required to go through any military lines to ride the train, to stay on the streets after 9 p.m., and to indicate your loyalty to the government. In order to obtain a pass, local citizens had to swear loyalty to the Constitution and laws that they would not give comfort or aid to the enemy. The penalty for violating this oath was death. On March 10, 1862, respected Bardstown businessman Joseph Hart was arrested by Colonel Jesse Bayles and Captain John Kurfiss of the 4th Kentucky for unstated crimes. Hart's family immediately asked Judge Linthicum to issue a writ of Habeas Corpus, which was ignored, and he was sent to the prison in Louisville. Hart was a police judge of Bardstown, a saddler by trade, and, after the war, sued the two officers for damages because of their actions.

Reverend John Atkinson was preaching at the Bardstown Methodist church during the time of the occupation of Bardstown by Federal troops. The provost Marshall Captain Jonathan Green issued an order in April that all the churches should be closed unless the pastors would "pray for the success of our army." Reverend Atkinson was known to be a Southern sympathizer and people were curious to know how he would get over the difficulty. When Sunday came, the Methodist church was opened as usual and a large crowd was in attendance, including Captain Green. Reverend Atkinson occupied the pulpit. In the course of his opening prayer, he asked a blessing on "our army" and prayed that it might be successful, adding in a lower voice, "Oh Lord, thou knowest which army I mean."

In September 1862, General Leonidas Polk of Bragg's Confederate Army was headquartered first in the Crozier house pictured above. Known as Culpepper and built by Benjamin Doom, it was a frame plantation house on the Springfield Pike where soldiers of different armies would water their horses at the spring over the hill.

The Left Wing of Bragg's Army was commanded by Major General William J. Hardee, whose headquarters at Bardstown were at Joseph Brown's house.

Bardstown continued to be occupied by the Union, though most of the training camps had emptied by May 1862. In August, the Loyalty Oath was required to be signed by jurors, common school commissioners, teachers, college professors, and ministers of Gospel before they could perform marriages.

In September 1862, General Braxton Bragg and the Army of the Mississippi came into Kentucky from Chattanooga, and Major General Kirby Smith invaded Kentucky from Knoxville. Smith continued on to Lexington. Bragg went the western route to Munfordsville, then turned east toward Bardstown. Lack of forage and food for the army was the reason to turn eastward instead of continuing toward the Union stronghold of Louisville, which was the original plan. General Don Carlos Buell's Army of the Ohio came from northern Alabama to try to outrun Bragg's army to Louisville. His march paralleled the Confederate army until Bragg turned toward central Kentucky.

After passing through New Haven, Bragg's troops arrived at Bardstown on September 22. They camped on all the main roads around the town. The right wing of the Army of the Mississippi was camped on the east side of town. Commanded by General Leonidas Polk, the headquarters were first at the Crozier house, then on the Murphy Farm on the Springfield Pike. Judge Felix Murphy lived at Maywood, the home of his wife's family about 3 miles out on the pike. The grounds were flat and fed by good springs, ideal for camps. General Benjamin Cheatham was put in command of the right wing with his headquarters on Mill Creek. The left wing was commanded by Major General William J.

Edgewood was the birthplace of Ben Hardin Helm in 1831. Helm was the brother-in-law of Abraham Lincoln and a general in the Confederacy. In 1862, Edgewood was the headquarters of General Braxton Bragg and General Leonidas Polk during the Confederate occupation of Bardstown.

Hardee, whose headquarters at Bardstown was at Joseph Brown's house just north of town. It was estimated that 28,000 troops were camped around the town.

On September 23, General Bragg asked for the use of the Saint Joseph College buildings on the same terms as the Union—monthly rent of $175. Father Verdin welcomed numerous former students from the ranks of Confederate troops. He was able to convince them to prepare their souls by confession. Shortly after this time, many of them were wounded or lost their lives at the Battle of Perryville, among them General Sterling A. Wood of Alabama.

On September 28, when General Braxton Bragg left Bardstown for Lexington to confer with General Kirby Smith, leaving General Polk in charge, Polk moved into Bragg's former quarters at Edgewood and took command of the whole army. When Polk and the Army of the Mississippi left Bardstown on October 3, their baggage train would be strung out for 10 miles.

Though Bardstown was occupied by the North and South at different times, only a few skirmishes occurred. The Battle at the Fairgrounds on October 4, 1862 was a clash between Union soldiers and the Confederates who were guarding the rear of Bragg's army moving to the east. A first-hand account of the fight was written for the *Confederate Veteran Magazine*. L.S. Ferrell, Company K, 4th Tennessee Cavalry soldier in the Fairgrounds fight, tells his story:

> When within a mile or two of Bardstown a rumor reached us that a heavy
> force of Federal Cavalry had slipped in between us and the town. Of

citizens who passed us some said there were no Federals between us and the town and others reported ". . . a Yankee line of battle across the pike at the fair grounds." To settle the question, Gen. (John) Wharton directed Capt. Anderson to take his company and ascertain the facts. We went at a gallop, and soon found them in line and "ready for business." Sending a courier hurriedly back to Gen. Wharton, Capt. Anderson called at the top of his voice "Form fours, my brave boys!" this was to mislead the enemy and gain a few precious moments of time. Meanwhile the Yankees began firing. They shot over our heads at first, but soon secured good range. The captain ordered the fence on our right pulled down so we could pass into a growth of timber. I sprang from my horse and lowered the fence. As the boys rushed through, one rode between me and my horse, and I was forced to turn him loose. The company kept right on and left me, striking the enemy's flank. Just then I wished that horse was somewhere else and I honorably with my wife and babies. Forty kingdoms would I have given for a horse, for my own little roan. I secured him with nerve, and just as I caught him I heard the hoof beat and muttering roar of Wharton's column as it advanced down the pike in a headlong charge "rough riders" they were, sure enough. . . .

Standing on his stirrups, bareheaded, his hair streaming behind, and whipping his gray mare Fanny across the withers with his hat, Gen. Wharton led the charge, shouting "Charge 'em, boys!" I fell in with the Texans.

When the head of our column struck the enemy the rail fence on our left went down in a moment, and we charged through an open woodland. Capturing a prisoner, Col. Tom Harrison ordered me to take him up behind me, and carry him to headquarters. As we had to retrace our steps and get on the pike to find headquarters, and as our forces had moved on and the Yankees were expected every minute, I thought it foolhardy to risk my prisoner with the advantage he would have behind me and for once disobeyed orders and made my prisoner double-quick. We had not proceeded very far when we encountered another Reb having charge of another prisoner. He asked me what I was going to do with my Yank. "Take him to headquarters," I replied. "Yes, and we will both be captured. I'm going to kill mine right here," he rejoined. At this the prisoner began begging for his life. I told Johnnie not to do so cowardly a deed as that, and requested him to turn his man over to me. "Take him and go to h—— with him!" he shouted, and, putting spurs to his horse was quickly out of sight leaving me with both prisoners, who readily ran until we were out of danger. . . .

By this headlong charge of Wharton's the Federals were scattered like chaff, and I think they lost about 15 in killed and wounded, and perhaps twenty-five or thirty prisoners. We had but one man wounded and that was slight. After the battle of Perryville we rode into Stanford. As we drew up in front of the hotel there were a group of paroled Federals on the verandah. Soon one of them sprang up, exclaiming: "Yonder's my man!" He ran to me and seizing my hand, seemed as glad as if he had found a long-lost brother. He was one of the Bardstown prisoners.

The Sisters of Charity and Nazareth Academy experienced many difficulties during the war. Many of their students were from the south or were of southern sympathies. The number of students decreased because of the conflict. Mother Columba wrote many times of the difficulties of normal life. Mail delivery, theft of their farm goods, difficulty in keeping help, fence rails used for soldiers' fires, and other problems.

Sister Marietta remembered:

> saucy Yankees in blue invaded. . . . They were the vanguard of Buell's army and were in hot pursuit of General Bragg. The boys in blue were very annoying, visiting the stable, dairy, etc, and pressing into service all they wished, were soon off. Mother Columba requested an officer to protect them from the insolence of these youths, but before discipline had been established, the soldier boys climbed on the outside of the window sills and taunted the girls who gave saucy retorts.

In the following months, the situation became so bad that she wrote Senator Lazarus W. Powell in Washington for help. His reply was an appeal to President Lincoln to consider her situation, the result being a written "safeguard" stating, "Let no depredation be committed on the property or possessions of the Sisters of Charity at Nazareth Academy near Bardstown, Ky. Jan. 17, 1865. A. Lincoln."

First Lieutenant H.W. Reddick of Florida wrote of his experiences while in the hospital at Bardstown with a severe fever:

> My room was on the third floor of the Female Academy which was used for a hospital and it fronted on the street so that I saw Buell's army as it passed through. I counted 110 flags. The wounded captured at Perryville were sent to the hospital at Bardstown and many of them died.

He was still there when the Confederates evacuated Bardstown. The school mentioned did not have a full third floor, but more likely had an attic space with dormer windows, as so many of the buildings had before the advent of electricity.

The most difficult period of any time during the war concerning Saint Joseph College were the days between October 5 and 17, 1862. By October 12, a total of 310 patients, 60 of whom were Confederate, were at the hospital. The following account is from the book *Jesuits of the United States*:

> There was much wrangling, at times even blows between the soldiers of North and South forced to live under the same roof. Some Union men

who had feigned sickness so as to be left behind at Bardstown . . . drank and quarreled with one another, rode roughshod over all the hospital regulations, stole the college poultry and vegetables and invaded the private apartments of the fathers, the officers being unable to control them. A sigh of relief was breathed by the Jesuits when on Oct. 17 some sixty or seventy of these undisciplined guests received their discharge from the hospital.

First Lieutenant H.W. Reddick of Florida told of his stay in the Bardstown hospital:

We fared very well while our army was in Bardstown but after it was captured by the Yankees, things were bad indeed. While our army was there, the ladies visited us, and did everything they could for us, but when the Yankees came in, this was not allowed and if it had not been for the Sisters of Charity we would have fared much worse. They did everything they could for us, and I for one will never forget their kindness.

The southern sympathizers of the town retreated into their stores and homes. Buell's army continued to pass through the town. In the second week of October, it is estimated that more than 5,000 Union soldier "stragglers," thought to be mostly "new troops" from the march of October 7 and 8, came "thronging"

Everyone leaving the town going east either to Bloomfield or Springfield must cross the bridge over Town Creek and turn right on the Springfield Pike or left for the Bloomfield Pike. All the soldiers passing through Bardstown on October 3-6 crossed over this bridge.

through Bardstown. By order of General Buell, "twice a day, stragglers were pushed through Bardstown at the point of the bayonet by the provost guard."

In late October, Governor Charles A. Wickliffe employed Joseph Z. Aud to carry the United States mail after the railroad trestles were destroyed by Bragg's troops. Aud drove a two-horse, six-passenger stage, which he said "sometimes carried up to 18 people, and was pulled by four horses." It was a tri-weekly mail. William F. Graves and Ben F. Wilson ran a stageline between Bardstown and New Haven during the same period. When the railroad was repaired and reopened in late February 1863, both stagelines went out of business.

General John H. Morgan came into Kentucky in December 1862, on what is now called the Christmas Raid. He captured Elizabethtown and its Federal garrison on December 27. His real target was the trestles on the Louisville and Nashville (L&N) Railroad at Muldraugh's Hill. He captured and burned them on December 28. Raiding parties destroyed the Cane Run bridge and two bridges on the Lebanon branch. He determined to head south. He was encamped on the

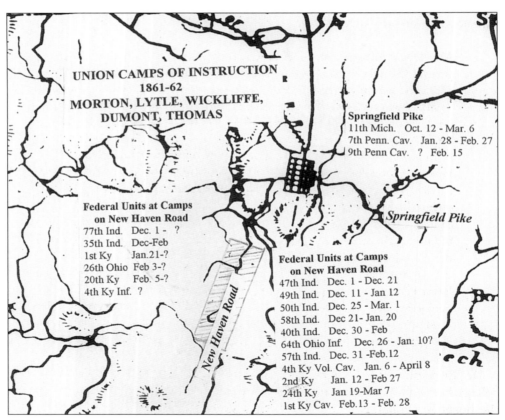

This 1862 map shows Bardstown and the roads leading from it. These lists indicate the Federal units that were at the Camps of Instruction. Most of the camps were south of town where the covered bridge prevented soldiers from slipping off into town without permission.

south bank of the Rolling Fork, still in Hardin County. The next morning, most of the force crossed into Nelson County at a ford a mile or two upriver from where the Elizabethtown-Bardstown road crossed the river. Morgan sent Colonel Cluke's regiment, with two pieces of artillery, on an operation 5 miles downriver to destroy a railroad bridge over the Rolling Fork. Colonel John Harlan and the federal troops caught up with the Rebels and opened fire with artillery as they were crossing the ford. They sent for Cluke and determined to defend the fords until he could return or his force would be stranded. The Rebels occupied a meadow, which had a sort of terrace running across it; this protected the men, but not the horses. The Rebels made a show of counter-attack, Cluke's regiment returned in good time, the Federals held back, and another good ford was discovered. The Rebels escaped the trap. They lost as captured one captain, one sergeant, and six privates. During the crossing of the river, Colonel Basil Duke was wounded in the head by a bursting artillery shell. He fell into the river, but was rescued, placed in a wagon commandeered from a nearby house, and brought to Bardstown to be treated.

Reverend John Cunningham was on hand when Duke was brought to Bardstown. Here are his words:

> About dark Morgan's men began to throng the streets. Among the arrivals was Brig. Gen. Basil Duke of Morgan's Division of Cavalry. He had been wounded in the short battle whose cannons' roar we had heard. It was necessary for him to be helped by others into the hall of Dr. Cox's two story brick house and up the stairway to the north end room, where he was laid on a thick pallet on the floor. Dr. Thomas Allen from nearby Taylorsville, a surgeon in Morgan's army, attended General Duke. I stood by and witnessed the treatment of the distinguished patient. The wound was on the right side of the head and when the doctor had washed the blood from it, I was invited to examine a cannon's work. The wound was supposed to be made by a small piece of bursted shell of a small cannon. A piece of the skin and bone behind the ear were gone. If the direction of the flying bit of shell had been directly from the right of the victim, it would have passed through the lower part of the head and death would have been instantaneous. As I bent over the prostrate warrior looking at his wound, he said in a somewhat cheerful tone, "that was a pretty close call." He did not complain or in any way indicate that his wound was a painful one.

On December 29, General Morgan entered Bardstown and occupied the college hospital. They took prisoner and paroled the 150 Federal soldiers left at the hospital. Morgan's men opened the county jail and freed several prisoners claiming to be Confederate sympathizers accused of stealing horses. Others burglarized the post office. The men also raided Bardstown businesses and left a bad taste even in the Confederate sympathizers' mouths over their behavior. In

May of 1863, the Federal authorities returned the college hospital to the Jesuits, everything clean and orderly "except for a few broken window panes."

The Jesuit fathers were in charge of the cathedral on January 15, 1863 when a Union regiment of Tennessee cavalry asked permission to use the church as a barracks. "Not withstanding the protests of its pastors, the church was seized by them and occupied but for two days only." Folklore had the pastor sending for Judge John Newman, "the Union man," to come and deal with the soldiers. Judge Newman dropped enough names of generals to convince the soldiers to take care in how they treated the church. Two days later, the regiment moved out of the church, leaving it quite undamaged.

Though the college had not had classes since the fall of 1861, in June of 1863, the Jesuits organized religion classes for the emancipated slaves. In the early classes, they had a small attendance of about 10 people. So, they introduced the singing of Catholic songs and hymns into the instruction programs. The African Americans began to frequent the classes in ever increasing numbers, 60 to 70 at a time. One of these, Daniel A. Rudd, the noted Catholic journalist, wrote that he had occasion as an adult to visit Reverend John Verdin in St. Louis. He called him "our old instructor" and wrote in the *American Catholic Tribune* that "it seemed like childhood days again when in Bardstown at old St. Joseph's we received words of counsel and listened to his matchless oratory." Since Saint Martha's was not built until after Rudd had left the community, Reverend Verdin must have impressed this young man at some of those religion classes and church sermons.

General John Hunt Morgan led his troops up from Tennessee in what became his Ohio Raid in July 1863. After fighting at Lebanon, he moved toward Bardstown. Forty-five troops from Morgan's First Cavalry CSA surrounded 26 Federals from the Fourth U.S. Cavalry in a livery stable at Bardstown. The skirmish lasted 20 hours and the Federals finally surrendered. A newspaper article 40 years later noted that Father Tom Major used to be known as Major Tom Major when he rode with Morgan. Noting that he had recently driven around the area, he related his memories of those times:

> When Nelson County was reached Capt. Ralph Sheldon was put in charge of twelve picked men to do some scout work, and that he was one of those twelve men; that, when near the fairgrounds, . . . they met twenty-six Union soldiers in the road; that they immediately fired upon the Yankees, and that the fire was quickly returned and a general fight ensued. The Yankees having twice as many men, compelled Sheldon's little squad to retreat, which they did in haste around the fairgrounds, through the Nazareth woods, and out by Hunter's Depot to the Shepherdsville road where they met some more of their men.

Then they rode into Bardstown, drove the Yankees into the livery stable now owned by George Conner, and kept them there all night. (The livery stable was on Lot #50 on the east side of north Third Street.) The next morning, the

This 1913 school parade picture shows the city hall building directly behind the car, the Christian church, and the livery stable in the background where Union soldiers held off General J.H. Morgan in the 1863 Civil War skirmish. The Central Hotel has been demolished.

Yankees, 31 in number under Captain Hynes, surrendered. Thirty of them were immediately paroled, but Captain Hynes, who had taken an oath never to take a Rebel soldier alive, was kept as a prisoner, and taken on towards Shepherdsville. Father Major says that, as they went along down the Shepherdsville road, Hynes riding a horse to himself, that the Rebel who had him in charge got a little further behind the command the further they went. He says there was great enmity in the command towards Captain Hynes because of the oath of cruelty he had taken and every man wanted the honor of shooting him. The man in charge of him fully intended to drop to the rear with him and kill him, but before this could be done, General Morgan learned that Hynes was in the rear in custody. His fears were aroused and, as Hynes had a brother who was a noble Confederate soldier, he determined to spare his life. He galloped to the rear, rode up to Hynes and said, "Mr. Hynes you are a free man, you are at liberty to go where you will." When General Morgan concluded, Hynes pointing to a Confederate said, "That fellow has my spur." General Morgan ordered the spur returned to Hynes and rode back to the head of his command as Hynes returned to Bardstown. Father Major said that Morgan did not dignify Hynes by addressing him as captain, but as Mr. Hynes, and showed his contempt for him by turning him loose without a parole.

"WICKLAND"—THE HOME OF THREE GOVERNORS

Julia Wickliffe Beckham's father was a staunch Unionist, but her brother John C. Wickliffe was serving in the Confederate army. A family story tells of her receiving a letter from John by a Confederate soldier at the side door of Wickland, when there was a knock on the front door—a Union soldier asking to search the grounds for a reported "Reb."

Bardstown was under martial law for almost all of the war years. The entire state suffered the loss of civil liberties as well as curtailed activities. During the election for governor in August 1863, the military governor ordered that only loyal citizens could vote. Former governor Charles A. Wickliffe was drafted by the Union Democrats to be their candidate for governor. He had worked to keep Kentucky from joining the South and later met to allow the Union to set up the camps, but at this point in the war, he was seen as being disloyal to the Constitution. On August 3, 1863, Colonel Thomas H. Butler of the Fifth Indiana Cavalry erased the name of Charles A. Wickliffe from the poll book in his presence and declared that no polling place in Kentucky was open to him even though he was a candidate for governor. They declared that he was disloyal to the Union.

Elections in Kentucky from 1799 until 1890 required the voter to come into the polling place and state their choice for the offices being elected. Several of the precincts in Nelson County received a written notice from the military commander of the county. The report of the elections officers in the August 3 election read:

> The judges, clerk and sheriff of District #5 in Nelson County met according to law and were served with an order from Colonel Butler to allow no names to go on the Poll Books except a list furnished by Capt. Leeson, acting under the foregoing military order and we were further

ordered by Capt. Leeson to proceed without the usual formality of an oath as required by the civil law. We therefore tender the foregoing report containing a list of the votes cast for the different candidates mentioned by the hands of Capt. Leeson to the clerk of the county court for the action of the proper officers. R.E. Horrell, Clerk.

Wickliffe attached a statement to the poll books that gave his position and proved his loyalty to the Constitution: "I deny that I am disloyal." *The Louisville Democrat* tried to report about these suppressed votes, but the Union-controlled press in Louisville made fun of these statements.

When Governor Wickliffe complained to the public through the *Louisville Journal*, Union reaction was "stop whining." Their investigation indicated "they had never saw an election more free from all military interposition and more open to voters of all parties." Collins's history notes differ, saying, "only about 85,000 out of 140,000 votes polled probably 40,000 being refused a vote, or kept from the polls by military intimidation or interference or by threats of arrest. . . . Regular Union candidates elected over the 'Independent Union' and over the Democratic candidates in every case."

A year later, the last week of August 1864, Wickliffe spoke at the Democratic Convention in Chicago:

> Many of the best and most loyal citizens of Kentucky—among them 20 or 30 ladies—are now imprisoned by the military in Louisville, in damp and dirty cells, with only straw to lie upon, and the coarsest fare. The newspapers of Louisville are forbidden to make the slightest allusion to this terrible state of affairs. I proclaim it here and now—at the risk of my liberty, perhaps of my life.

His daughter Julia Wickliffe Beckham had a heart-wrenching time during the war. Her father, ex-governor C.A. Wickliffe, was a staunch Unionist, but her brother John C. Wickliffe had joined the First Kentucky Brigade CSA in September 1861. A family story tells of her answering a knock on the side door of the home and receiving a letter from John by a Confederate soldier, while a loud knock at the front door was a Union soldier asking to search the grounds for a reported "Reb."

It was the fourth year of occupation of Bardstown; most of the Union troops and war action had moved south, but the North was drafting soldiers from Kentucky. The same William Carothers who tried to run off and join Morgan three years before wrote about the draft in his journal. On September 18, 1864 a draft was held at Lebanon. Carothers directed his friend to notify him, if he was drafted, to send a telegraph saying, "You are not drafted."

> Mr. White the telegraph operator came to my house at midnight. I was sleeping over Baker Smiths' Store where I was employed and when he

knocked I looked out the window. "I have good news for you, You are not drafted." With a sinking heart I hastily dressed and went home packed my trunk and had it sent to Nazareth (depot) and kissing my mother and sisters goodbye and promising to write, I hastened to the depot to catch the morning train for Louisville. Took on my trunk at Nazareth and at half past eight reached Louisville in safety. I visited the rooms for substitutes and found I couldn't get one for less than $2500 which I thought was excessive and I didn't have the money. I exchanged my greenbacks into gold and purchased a ticket from Jeffersonville to New York.

Adventures crossing the Ohio, catching the train, and avoiding the military checking passes brought Carothers to New York. He looked up Reverend Nathan L. Rice, former president of Roseland Academy and the Carothers's next-door neighbor at Bardstown. He was now the pastor of the Brick Presbyterian Church, "the wealthiest church in the United States." On October 15, Carothers took Dr. Rice's advice and left New York for Canada. Dr. Rice accompanied him to the railroad station and gave him $10 in gold, saying it was done for the love of his parents and for good luck.

On October 20, Carothers got a job with an "old Frenchman dairy farmer," who offered to pay him $14 a month to milk for him. Carothers stuck it out for three weeks, then went back to job searching. Locating a man who resembled him in appearance, he proposed to have him, William Marcus Butler, take out papers for the United States. Carothers obtained a certificate as a British subject under the name of William Marcus Butler and, under this name, crossed over the border traveling to Pennsylvania. On November 15, he was at the home of his father's brother Abraham. Visiting around his relatives and helping on the different farms took up most of the time until January. He went to prayer meetings, tried to get a job on the Pennsylvania Railroad, and searched the newspaper ads for positions. Discouraged and far from home, he wrote, "I was greatly surprised at receiving a letter from home with my dear mother's ambrotype . . . the image is not equal to the original." He traveled to Philadelphia in January, trying to find work, had his money stolen from his trunk, worked as a streetcar conductor until some soldiers tried to shoot him for putting them off the car, and also worked in the repair shop at the streetcar company. When applying for a job, he was asked if he was a Presbyterian. He presented a letter from "Reverend Joe McDonald, the blind preacher," who called him "his elder" as a reference for a government job. On February 1, he went to Washington for work. He returned home after the war and entered into business with his brother, who also survived the war.

The Civil War created opportunities to settle old feuds and bad blood. Those men who would ignore the law in peacetime used the war opportunity to steal and destroy under the guise of supporting a cause. In September of 1864, coming directly from New Haven where they had burned the depot, "Henry Magruder and eight of his guerillas are in Bardstown where they captured the telegraph operator, demolished his instrument and stole his personal effects," reported the *Louisville Journal*.

W.J. Nelson wrote in *The Kentucky Standard* in 1938 of his knowledge of the guerillas:

> In the fall of 1864, One Arm Berry assembled about 300 of his men in the streets of Fairfield, and marched on three roads to Bardstown and attacked a garrison of federal troops barricaded in the courthouse. After some maneuvering, they surrounded the garrison and opened the fight. They were repulsed, several killed and many wounded, among them was One Arm Berry shot through.

Taken to a private home near Fairfield, he was secretly treated and slowly recovered.

Three months later, guerrillas were responsible for the murder of two officers of the Seventh Pennsylvania Cavalry at the home of W.R. Grigsby on the Springfield Pike near Bardstown. The *Pottsville* (Pennsylvania) *Miners Journal* of January 14 reported:

On September 19, 1864, William Carothers of Bardstown received the coded message that he had been drafted in the Union Army. He determined to escape Kentucky and the draft, and returned after the war to become a successful merchant.

On Thursday afternoon, while the Seventh Pennsylvania cavalry were approaching Bardstown, Ky., Capt. R. McCormick, AAG on the colonel's staff and Major John L. Shirk, Surgeon of the regiment, went into the house of a Mr. Grigsby, one mile out of town. Major Shirk was acquainted with the family, and not having seen them for some time, concluded to pay them a friendly visit.

(He had camped on their farm during the time the unit was in the Camp of Instruction at Bardstown in 1862.)

They had been there but a few minutes, and Mr. Grigsby's daughter was entertaining them with a song at the piano, when an African-American woman rushed into the room. However, upon seeing the officers, she rushed out again. Miss Grigsby followed her out, but she came back hurriedly and before she could tell the officers of the danger they were in, the house was surrounded by Sue Mundy and 15 guerrillas, who fired upon them through the windows and doors, but did not succeed in hitting any of them. Mr. Grigsby went to the door and informed the guerillas that there were but two soldiers in his house and that they would surrender, but they pushed him to one side, rushed in, and murdered both

In September 1864, guerillas intended to burn the depot, but were treated to some "fine old whiskey, and a present of some jars of delicious pickles" by the railroad agent and went away without damaging the building.

of them on the spot. Congressman Ben Johnson wrote in a history column in the 1930s that it was Babe Hunter, not Mundy, who led the guerillas.

When the Bardstown soldiers came back after the war, they tried to forget the horror and the losses. The defeated Confederates wanted to get on with their lives. The Union veterans were in the minority in the community, but they were on the winning side. In the years ahead in Kentucky, the "Bourbon Democrats," former Confederate officers or sympathizers, would emerge as the political party of strength and several Bardstown veterans participated in the new wave of office holders. For the next 30 years, the Democrats held the public offices in Kentucky.

After many letters, conferences, and prayers, the Jesuits left the college and turned it back to the diocese. Lack of priests and non-ownership of the land were the deciding reasons to not reopen the school. There was no money given to them for the improvements or land purchased. The items existing at the school, vestments belonging to the "parochial Church," books, beds, bedding, and other items, there when it was acquired by the Jesuits in 1848, were returned. Any books purchased by the society, and all vestments and paintings in the "domestic chapels," belonged to the society, as did the livestock and all debts due to the college that could be collected. The college was returned to the diocese free of debt in December 1868.

On a fair day in October 1869, the students of Saint Thomas marched on foot to Bardstown while their trunks were carried on big wagons that formed part of the cortege. They numbered about 60 and nearly one-third were from Indiana. Kentucky students were the second numerous and little Rhode Island was third. They found good teachers and kind fathers at Saint Joseph.

4. Progress, Patriotism, and Public Spirit, 1870–1900

Looking back at this 30-year period, it appears that political leadership was somewhat subdued, but Jesse James and moonshining kept the lawmen hopping. Citizens of Bardstown demanded lights, clean streets, and a city hall. The county officials built a new jail and a new courthouse. Schools continued to turn out educated leaders for the community. Fires were fought and churches were built or renovated. People of all ages were entertained in all seasons. The Kentucky spirit, bourbon, was being made and shipped out to markets all over the country.

Only three copies of three different newspapers from 1860 until 1875 survive to provide information about the events of that period in Bardstown. The *Nelson County Record* began publication in 1875 and continued until 1905. With 25 percent of the copies surviving, it provided a variety of information about the latter part of the nineteenth century. In 1888, the wife of the *Nelson County Record* newspaper editor, Mrs. John P. Murray, contributed to *Woman's Illustrated World*, published in Philadelphia. In 1884, her novel *Aunt Sarah's Ward* was serialized in 16 issues of the *Nelson County Record*. The *Bardstown Local Item* was listed as being published in 1880, but none of the copies survive.

Many other people contributed to the literary history of this period, including Reverend Jouett Vernon Cosby. He was an educator and poet. His poem "Consecration" was published in pamphlet form in April 1874. Mrs. Sarah Irvin Mattingly founded the *Kentucky Magazine* at Bardstown in 1880. She was the second wife of Dr. C.P. Mattingly and "was the first woman editor of an American magazine devoted to literature and science." Judge John E. Newman was the author of *Newman's Pleadings and Practice* in 1884, which is found in many law libraries. His wife Marian Olive Newman wrote poetry. Ben J. Webb was the editor of *The Catholic Advocate* in Bardstown in the 1830s and when it moved to Louisville, he established the *Catholic Guardian* in 1858. In 1884, he published the *Centenary of Catholicity in Kentucky*, a great work of Catholic history.

The hotels were the same buildings of decades ago, but with different owners. The two-story hotel on north Third Street (Lot #49) was called the Ellis House in the late 1870s. In the lobby of this hotel, in 1881, Jesse and Frank James narrowly missed being arrested by detectives Yankee Bligh and George Hunter. The detectives brought two others for reinforcement as they went into the hotel,

The most famous police detective of the era, George W. Hunter, began his career in 1868 as a marshall of Bardstown at $50 per month. After retiring as town marshall, he captured many wanted men and solved many crimes in this period of history.

but local sheriff Donnie Pence and Ben Johnson joined the James brothers. Jesse walked through the lobby with his arms crossed over his chest and his hands under his coat. He turned and stood while the others walked out the door. After they brought the horses from the nearby livery stable, they quickly mounted and left. Knowing a gunfight would be deadly, the detectives backed off and the James boys rode away.

Ellis Hall was the location, in 1880, of the Mississippi Minstrels show in July, and December entertainment included drama, tableaux, music, and other features to benefit Saint Joseph Church. "The Aid Society of the Methodist Church will give a candy pulling November 15th in the dining room at the Ellis House." Part of this hotel was an accepted public exhibition room for the tee-totaling Methodists to use. It was also used by school teacher Mrs. Walker for the public school examination of small children, assisted by Miss Hayden and Miss Potts. In 1882, the Ellis House became the Central Hotel, operated by S. Graham. Two years later, I.M. Hughes owned it when "a lot of plaster fell from the ceiling. Owen Ellis was struck by it and was laid up for a couple of days. The chandelier and showcase were broken."

In June 1880, the young men of Nelson County gave a Hop at the Hynes House with music by Eichorn's Band. Three years later, the Newman House,

If you ignore the street lights and highway signs, you would see the Newman House as it looked c. 1885. Shady Bower, Hynes House, Newman House—it was known by many names until finally, in 1912, it was called the Talbott Hotel.

formerly Hynes House, was owned by T.O. and W.H. Newman. They sold it to the partnership of Isaac Hughes, George M. Talbott, and Ben Talbott in 1885. Later, Hughes sold his share to G.M. Talbott and Brother. Talbott determined to lease the Newman House for $800 for one year in the fall of 1889 to "Mr. Frank Kearns and William Jones of Lebanon, for $800. The lessees also to board G.M. Talbott and family until March 1st. Talbott & Bro. retained the livery stable which will probably be conducted by G.M. Talbott while Mr. Ben Talbott will get into something else." By 1893, only George Talbott was operating the Newman House.

Thomas Beam, D.M. Beam, and James B. Beam operated Old Tub Saloon, a coffee house at Black's Hotel on north Third. In 1890, they erected a whisky barrel with "Old Tub" painted on it as a sign for their business. After receiving complaints, the trustees requested they remove it, but agreed to wait until after the fair in September.

It was announced in April 1893 that the newly reopened Bardstown Hotel (the old Central Hotel), with T.D. Beam as proprietor, and T.H. Ellis and Morgan McIsaac as clerks, had been thoroughly renovated with new furniture. Eight months later, the Bardstown Foot Ball Club sponsored a Christmas Hop at the hotel. In the same month and at the same place, ".a unique entertainment will be given for the benefit of the Methodist Church. All the ladies present will be masked."

A cholera epidemic threatened the community in the fall of 1873; the town marshal was directed not to grant any license to any shows or exhibitors until further notice. It was also asked that the Nelson County Agricultural Association be requested to postpone their fair from the first week in September until the threat of sickness was over. Melon sales were prohibited because of the illness.

The Nelson County fairs were grand occasions. Special excursion trains ran from Louisville filled with fairgoers. They enjoyed horse shows and musical entertainment, and they cheered for their favorites in the foot and bicycle races. It was announced that the fair company had purchased a large street sprinkler to use during the event to keep down the dust. The Louisville Legion Band provided "the best music ever heard at the Nelson Fair." A dividend of $3 in tickets on each share of stock in the Nelson County Agricultural Association was declared by the board of directors. These "free tickets" brought families out to meet their friends at the fair. "Floral Hall is a great anxiliary to the success of the Fair. . . . Our county ladies, young and old, all have various articles they could enter for prizes, and many they could lend to decorate the Hall and make it attractive."

Another type of horse show was held in the spring of 1887 when horsemen from far and wide gathered along the two blocks south of the courthouse on Third Street. They were displaying the finest show and breeding horses around. Spectators lined the streets to inspect and select for breeding purposes horses from Nelson and surrounding counties. One intrepid owner hired a brass band

T.D. Beam took over the Bardstown Hotel and operated the Old Tub Saloon there in 1896. Son of David Beam and brother of Jim Beam, he promoted his family's whiskey.

OLD TUB
SALOON

OLD TUB
WHISKY

I have for sale BOONE & BRO.'s Three-year-old. Strictly Pure, 40c. per quart.
Also F. G. Walker's "QUEEN OF NELSON" Four-year-old, 50c per quart.

OLD · TUB · WHISKY

Three years and up, 60 to 75c per quart, guaranteed Strictly Pure, just as it is when taken from bonded warehouse.
Keeps the best brand of Brandies, Wines, Cigars, Tobacco; also ice cold Beer and Ale.

T. D. BEAM, Prop.

and tied ribbons and banners to the harness of his steeds to attract the attention of the public.

The Ladies of the Monument Association were trying to raise funds to purchase a monument for the Confederate graves, and a Fourth of July picnic, in 1896, had been advertised for several weeks:

> The picnic on the 4th at the college grounds bids fair to be one of the most enjoyable occasions ever held in Bardstown. The enthusiastic spirit which all connected with the arrangements have shown cannot fail to make it one grand success. The distinguished speakers having kindly consented to deliver the addresses, should alone be sufficient to attract a very large audience. A bicycle will be awarded to the most popular lady on the ground, this to be determined by vote of those present. Among the amusing features will be a cakewalk and potato races. A good band of music will be in attendance; also the military and fire companies will take part, altogether making this a gala occasion. The entire net proceeds to be devoted to the erection of a monument in the Confederate lot in the Bardstown Cemetery.

Businesses advertised that they would close between noon and 5 p.m. so everyone could attend the picnic:

> Lets everybody attend the picnic tomorrow. You can't afford to miss it, there will be more fun to the square inch than any place you ever struck. Good times are coming. Go down to the College Grounds tomorrow, turn your money loose, help out a noble patriotic cause and you will never regret it.

The college grounds were now the Saint Thomas orphanage grounds. Every orphan must have been hard to control from excitement.

Called by many the "Confederate Picnic," a parade preceded the program at 9:30 a.m. with the Nelson County Rifles and the fire department, all headed by the Fairfield Band. Balloting for the most popular young lady to receive the Cleveland bicycle began at 10 a.m. and closed at 6 p.m. Band music and tennis games filled in between the formal program and the speeches. Refreshments of all kinds were furnished at low prices.

Many types of games and races were held: potato races, shoe races, hurdle races, sack races, three-legged races, and wheelbarrow races. The cakewalk and clog dancing were entertaining for all. It was announced ahead of time that the Louisville train would be held for picnic attendees.

In January 1897, one could have attended two types of entertainment of opposite attractions. The first was the prize fight of African-American fighters Isaac Barrett of Louisville and Tom Collins of Bardstown. "They engaged in a bout in which Collins succeeded in knocking out Barrett in six rounds. This is a

This pre-1890 view of the business area shows that it hadn't changed much since the Civil War. A few more brick buildings replaced frame ones. The Caldwell yellow house on the left and the Grinstead Produce store on the right were replaced in 1900 by the Johnson Building and James M. Wilson's Drugstore.

great card in favor of Collins, as Barrett is a pugilist of some reputation. David Tutt was the referee." The second was a less heated affair. The river as well as all the ponds and smaller streams were frozen over and large crowds of young people were out skating every day. "Mr. E.L. Bowman has acted as chaperone to several parties. Mrs. Bowman is a graceful skater and is very fond of the sport."

Joseph Muir writes about his youthful experiences in 1896 and 1897 when his friends had a "Century Club," which meant they rode 100 miles on a 65-pound bicycle in one day, up and down hills and over rough roads. The following was reported on the event:

> At first there were enrolled Will Wilson, Mat Evans, Les Samuels, Sam Carothers, Columbus Cherry, and "Brother Gypie" Mattingly, John Grundy and Myself. We had speedometers on our wheels—set at "0." We left Bardstown at 5 am—went first in one direction and the next Sunday in another direction. Hodgenville & E-town, Springfield & Lebanon, etc. Louisville, Bloomfield, Chaplin, Frankfort. Those were the routes all summer on Sundays. Will Wilson rode the season out, as did Sam Carothers, Mat Evans & myself. Les Samuels stuck it out for a few trips. "Gyp" Mattingly died and Sam Carothers died during the winter. Cherry and Grundy started two or three times, but turned back after a few miles. I was about 18 years of age, weighed about 125 lbs. and had a Cleveland Bike—which weighed 65 lbs. Oh my legs and back!

Bardstown leaders had big dreams for the growth of the community when they made a proposal for the Central University to be built here. They were competing with Richmond and Paris for the school. They proposed the Federal Hill land for the site and promised other funding, but they came up short. The following was reported:

> In 1873 the Alumni Association of Central University met at Richmond for the purpose of choosing a site for the University. Richmond, Bardstown and Paris had proposed land and money for the location. Richmond had $101,355 in cash and interest, Bardstown $60,600 of which cash was $53,600 and land $7000. From Paris $140,000, cash subscriptions and interest $100,000 in guaranteed building fund, $10,000, income from the Garth Fund worth $30,000. Richmond was chosen by a vote of 217, Paris 177, Bardstown 10.

In 1879, the local schools were recognized by the *Church & Home Publication*: Bardstown Public School had 100 students; Roseland had 45; Male & Female had 70; the public school for African Americans had 45; Saint Joseph College had 65; Saint Martha's, also for African Americans, had 60; Bethelehem Institute had 75; and Nazareth had 115. "For educational advantages Bardstown is unsurpassed by any town of its size in the country."

Mrs. Rebecca Rowan's home, known as Federal Hill when built by her father-in-law in 1800–1819, and now called "My Old Kentucky Home" by those familiar with the family relationship to Stephen C. Foster, sits quietly on the hill east of Bardstown.

The Saint Martha's Colored School was one of the last gifts of the Jesuits. They taught religion classes for the freed slaves at Saint Joseph College in 1863. Three years later, after consulting with Bishop Spalding, they collected money from the Chicago area and locally, and $1,600 was set aside to build a church and school for the emancipated slaves. It was erected by 1871 and operated as Saint Martha's School by the Sisters of Charity. In the Christmas season in 1877, an advertisement read, "the Colored ladies will have a festival at St. Martha's Colored School on December 26, 27 all invited to benefit institution. Ten cents admission."

Enrollment was down at Roseland Academy at this time, but Mrs. J.V. Cosby continued the school and, in 1894, held a fundraising event:

> A pleasant house will be guaranteed to all who will attend the book sale at the Academy tomorrow night at 8 o'clock. Admission 15 cents and refreshments furnished without charge. Proceeds will be applied to repairs of the Academy building.

The funds did not keep the school from closing in 1895 and, three years later, Roseland Academy became Nelson County Normal School. As the Normal School, it offered courses to prepare students for the teaching profession. "Nelson County Normal School will begin 20th for ten weeks courses. Private Board $2. Per week. Bed at the best hotel in town $3 per week. Edgar Crawford Principal."

During the war with Spain in 1898, a flag-raising was held at the Presbyterian Academy under the auspices of Professor Crawford and faculty of the Bardstown Normal School. This school, begun in 1844 on the east side of south Third Street, has a long list of names. A private Protestant institution, it was managed by a Methodist church board of trustees and was known as the Bardstown Female Institute. Taken over by the Baptists in 1865, it was called the Baptist Female College. It had financial difficulties and the school was opened to boys in 1876 as Bardstown Male and Female Institute. Finally in 1904, it was named the Bardstown Co-educational College. The school officially closed in 1908. In the early 1890s, it was affiliated with Georgetown College. In 1891, it listed seven teachers and the claim, "True Home School with ample accommodations and R.H. Stone as Principal."

It was known as the Male and Female Institute when Professor Robert N. Cook was principal from 1896 to 1898. "Prof. Cook to Chaperone party to Mammoth Cave. Railroad fare, hotel bill, ride fee, round-trip is $7.80. Leave on Friday return next day." This school was later known as the Bardstown Baptist Institute and was torn down.

On September 11, 1884, Bardstown Public School opened with 80 pupils. Professor Edgar Crawford was the teacher in 1890. A teachers' library was set up for county teachers in 1896 under Superintendent Morgan Yewell. They could take one book for three weeks. There were 81 volumes added in 1898.

Newspaper accounts of activities at Saint Joseph College in the 1870s have the most information for a researcher about this period in the school's history. In

1879, an account of the celebration of Washington's birthday was dismal: "Nothing but rain, down it poured as if the floodgates of heaven were open anew, . . . not allowing the projected athletic outdoor sports in which prizes were to be given those who might visibly demonstrate their superior agility and muscular power." Celebrations of the Feast of Saint Joseph and Fourth of July were reported in great detail. The contribution of the students in speeches and music was particularly noted.

The *Nelson County Record,* in August 1880, announced the school opening on September 6 for reception of pupils, both Catholic and non-Catholic. One session lasted ten months. The course of studies embraced the classical and commercial branches. Board, tuition, washing, and other amenities cost $200 per session. There was a physicians's fee of $5.

People were to contact and apply to the president for details. One week after the opening, Bishop McCloskey sang a Pontifical mass in the new chapel. This time-honored institution opened with 75 students, all told, and President Mackin hoped, before the close of the month, to have 100 scholars within the walls of old Saint Joseph.

The halfway point in this 20 year operation of the school was reached by the June 1880 commencement of Saint Joseph College. A stand erected in the yard adjoining the college prepared seats for several hundred people. At 10 a.m., Bishop McCloskey and the clergy, followed by the military company, took their places and the exercises opened. Speeches and band music followed with some solo performances on the violin and melodeon.

"St. Joseph's College, The Great Institution of Learning to be Closed" read the headlines on the article in the *Nelson County Record* of August 29, 1889:

> Few announcements of this character would be received at this place with so many expressions of sorrow as this one. It not only robs us of much of our prestige as an educational center, but it materially affects the business of the town and vicinity—besides the lack of opportunity to give a collegiate education to the young men of the town.

The faculty were caught off guard, but Professor C.K.J. Peterson advertised, "St. Joseph College having been closed for approaching season. I will now have time and would like to get a class of music pupils. I also teach French and German. I can teach vocal music and also to play upon any instrument." Professor Schaedler planned to go to Louisville or Saint Mary's. The article expressed the hope that the school would soon be reopened.

Each time the school changed hands or closed for some period of time, the community, Catholic and Protestant, let their unhappiness be known. Often, this show of community support helped those in control make positive decisions. But no effort by the faithful or City Fathers succeeded in reopening the school.

Three months before Saint Joseph College closed, fire destroyed the orphanage building at Saint Thomas operated by the Sisters of Charity since 1872. The vacant college buildings were offered for the orphanage. The orphans moved from Preston Park in Louisville to Bardstown in 1891. They occupied this campus until September of 1910 when they moved back to Louisville.

Bardstown Baptist Church on Lot #50 was destroyed by fire for the second time in 1891. This time, the congregation determined to build at another location. E.B. Smith was chosen to design the new church on Lot #9. By late 1891, an article stated that the Baptist church was progressing, with "Thomas B. Joyce doing the stonework." The church was completed by March 28, 1893 when they requested permission from the city trustees to fill the baptistry at their new church from the public cisterns.

After an extensive fund drive in the late 1880s, the African Methodist Episcopal Zion Church had begun to build a new building. On December 10, 1891, "the Church which was in course of erection was blown down by wind . . . They had been endeavoring to raise money to cover it, but the desired amount had not been obtained."

The newspaper reported the following:

> The Presbyterians raised over $2,200 to pay off their debt on their church and parsonage, in the spring of 1893, and will spend the rest on enclosing their church yard with an iron fence, sodding, and putting a cement pavement in front. [The Presbyterians met in the Methodist Church several times when their building was in disrepair.] The Methodist are not going to be behind—We understand they want to raise $5,000 to remodel

The 1879 Saint Joseph College's Cornet Band posed in front of Flaget Hall Classroom building. They provided music at the Feast of Saint Joseph at the Cathedral.

This interior view of Saint Joseph Cathedral reflects the 1879 renovation. Elaborate wooden altar surrounds of carved trim and wooden urns framed the painting "The Crucifixion" and the statues in each side altar. The Episcopal throne on the left of the sanctuary and an elevated pulpit on the right were retained from the earlier church.

the entire interior and build a spire. Mr. Osso Stanley has submitted plans and figures which are generally favored by the congregation. Reverend David Morton, minister of the Methodist church, encouraged the addition of the steeple and installing the art glass windows.

In the 1880s, church activities ranged from the candy pulling at J.B. Brown's store on a Saturday afternoon and an oyster supper at night sponsored by the ladies of the Methodist Episcopal Church South to the "dime supper" given by the children in the Presbyterian church. The supper was to be sold in dime parcels and the proceeds were used for charitable purposes.

Under the leadership of Father C.J. O'Connell, Saint Joseph Cathedral underwent renovation. The newspaper reported in December of 1877, "A subscription was taken up in the Cathedral last Sunday to provide heaters for the church. We understand about $1,000 was subscribed."

The first major change was the renovation of 1879. Elaborate wooden altar surrounds of carved trim and wooden urns framed the painting "The

Crucifixion" and the statues in each side altar. The Episcopal throne on the left of the sanctuary and an elevated pulpit on the right were retained from the earlier church. However, the original stone altar was replaced by dropping the 3,000-pound, 10-foot by 2-foot by 1-foot stone below the floor of the sanctuary. In 1882, Max Leber was employed to cover the whitewashed ceiling and walls with decorative painting. The following was reported on the renovation:

> A recent addition has been made to St. Joseph's Church in 1884 in the shape of five life-size marble statues—St. Joseph, St. Mark, St. Luke, St John and St. Matthew. The statues were presented by the following persons: Mrs. Stocker & Hurst, Henry Edelin, Mrs. P.S. Barber and Mrs. J.W. Muir. A new and beautiful Baptismal Fount was presented by Mr. Frank Shader.
>
> Saint Joseph's Church is now one of the most beautiful in the country. The paintings, statuary and frescoing give it the appearance of a European Cathedral.

Jacob Hast, born in Bavaria in 1830, died in Bardstown in June 1854. He taught drawing and painting at Saint Joseph College. The above painting, "The Immaculate Conception," hangs in the cathedral.

The county court also began expanding the government buildings. In 1874, the county court determined to build a new jail adjoining the old one. A tax was passed to raise funds and the stone cell block was constructed. The jailer lived in the old 1820 jail and housed prisoners in the new cell block. A stone wall was constructed around the lot, making a work yard for the prisoners. This building was used until 1986 as the jail for Nelson County. Today, it continues to furnish room and board—now to tourists who stay at the Jailers Inn Bed and Breakfast.

In 1891, the county judge and fiscal court decided to advertise for designs for a new courthouse. It was to be designed to accommodate all the county offices and the courtroom in one building, eliminating the need for the brick county office building in front of the jail. At a meeting at Bardstown of the Farmers Alliance of Nelson County (membership 525), the group put up resolutions opposing building a new courthouse in this county. The resolutions were presented to the magistrates of this county for them to take action on at their next meeting. They

After 1874, the Nelson County jailer lived in the old 1820 jail and housed prisoners in the new cell block. A stone wall was constructed around the lot, making a work yard for the prisoners.

The new Nelson County Courthouse was designed in the Richardsonian Romanesque style by Maury and Dodd of Louisville. When the contract was signed in 1892 for the construction, the court directed that stones from the old building be used in the foundation of the new one.

also appointed a committee to "do something in regard to our turnpike system in some way or other."

A larger court building was needed to accommodate the increasing court business and to provide safety vaults for the volume of county archives. An architectural design competition was held and the design of Mason Maury and William J. Dodd of Louisville was chosen. It was designed in the Richardsonian Romanesque style, to be built of stone and brick with wood framing. When the contract was signed with Edward B. Smith Jr. for construction, the court directed that stones from the old building be used in the foundation of the new one. In April 1891, W.C. Lyons, one of the contractors for the building, requested permission from the trustees to construct rails from the depot down Third to the courthouse for the moving of freight and materials in horse-drawn cars. After conferring with the businessmen along the route, permission was granted to construct it south on Third to Chestnut, west on Chestnut to Mulberry Alley, then south on the alley to Market, then east to the courthouse site. This didn't interfere with downtown business. This agreement was for 100 days of use. This same track was used by the builders of the new Baptist church later in the year. The courthouse was completed for use by 1893 and cost $33,000 furnished.

In 1882, the city trustees purchased 50 coal-oil street lamps and erected them along the city streets. Immediately, a law was passed imposing a fine of $5 for injuring or breaking any of these. W.A. Taylor was hired as the first lamplighter. Later, the trustees hired two lamplighters because the time it took one person to

Wigginton, Boone and Company was located on the northeast corner of Arch and Third Streets. They sold furniture, carpets, and coffins. The combination of furniture sales and undertaking was common. A man is standing on the cistern cover. The cisterns were used for fire protection water.

start at one end of town and light all the lamps shortened the time the lights were on in the part of the town farthest away from the beginning. The lamplighter had to return and extinguish each lamp after a certain time. On nights when the moon was full, the lamps weren't lit. In 1890, two young men, J. Harrell Jr. and Eddie Coomes, bid $144 on the job of lighting the street lamps. Later, rules were passed prohibiting hitching horses to the lamp posts, and carving or whittling on the wooden posts.

The trustees heard reports from the fire company about their equipment needs: a new double connector for the engine hose; a new bell for the fire company, which had "to be between 1 and 200 pounds more than the present one in use"; work needed on the engine; and work needed on the engine house. The city took bids to rebuild the "cupalo" on the engine house. John F. Smith worked on the "belfry" of the engine house for a fee of $24. The bell was purchased for $152.57 and the old bell sold. The trustees also purchased 500 feet of "Eureka Hose" for the use of the town.

In 1879, the wardens of the fire company complained that the cisterns in town were full of mud, indicating a shortage of water storage for fire fighting. In the 1880s, Jordall Hall and John Donohoo worked as messengers of the fire company for $100 year. In September 1885, a new fire engine was purchased of Ahren Steam Fire Engine Manufacturing Company of Cincinnati for $900. Three months later, a new fire company was organized as Bardstown Fire Company No. 2. A committee appointed to report a plan to dry the fire department hose reported that Cox, Moore & Whelan would do the work for $65. They also paid Elzie Russel to work on the fire engine in November.

The trustees passed a law in September 1895 that, to promote fire safety, all buildings in the city of Bardstown should be roofed with slate, tile, or metal, or the residents would be subject to a $100 fine.

A rash of fires in the fall of 1884 strained the fire company's resources. In September, Mrs. Rebecca Rowan's residence caught fire, but it sustained little damage.

In November, the livery stable of G.M. Talbott and Brother, adjoining the Newman House, was fired by an incendiary and almost completely destroyed. The newspaper reported the following:

> The fire company was soon at the scene and by splendid work checked the flames, and prevented their spread to the hotel which was in great danger. It was with the greatest exertion that the hotel was saved. Blankets and comforts were spread on the roof and kept wet with water. The large frame shed between the stable and the hotel burned like tinder and at one time it looked as if the hotel could not be saved. But the brave firemen fought back the flames and not only saved the hotel, but a large part of the shed. Sparks fell on the roof of the Courthouse and set it afire. Ed. Hickman climbed on the roof and extinguished the flames or Nelson County would have had to build a new temple of justice. The horses were saved but several of the young men who were trying to save them were overcome with smoke.
>
> The next night the Colored Church (Union Church) on Second street was fired by an incendiary, by placing combustible material between an outside shutter and the window. The shutters, window and frame burned and made such a bright light that it was discovered and extinguished. The building is brick and the flames did not extend far enough to destroy it. Had it been frame it would have been a total loss.

Subsequent issues of the *Nelson County Record* reported on the investigation:

> A Committee was formed to investigate the various acts of incendiarism about town—the officers of the law had evidence in their possession and had announced their purpose to make several arrests, but the same has not been done. It is expected that the next Grand Jury will thoroughly examine into the matter. Locals are enraged against them. They are walking on a mine, and it will take but little to explode it. For the sake of the good name of our town and through sympathy for the innocent hearts that will be crushed, we hope that those who have fallen into evil ways will realize their danger before it is everlastingly too late.

A citizen who attended the meeting reported that there was an effort being made by friends of the alleged incendiaries to turn it into a whitewashing committee and that he would attend no more.

As if there was not enough panic about fires, two weeks later, the kitchen of Professor Greenwell's school building caught fire from a defective flue and the main building narrowly escaped destruction. However, by the quick and effective work of the young men of the school and of the town who formed a "bucket brigade," it was saved. The hook-and-ladder department soon placed their ladders against the burning kitchen and, with the many buckets used about the school, the flames were subdued without using the engine. The kitchen was a frame structure and the flames spread quickly. At one time, the roof of the main building was on fire and it looked as if it would be destroyed. A panic spread among the pupils and they began throwing things out the windows at a rapid rate.

In the fall of 1880, a campaign was begun in the newspaper for a "capacious town hall." It was suggested that a joint stock company be formed to build a large hall for commencements and other events. The paper asked that a public hearing be held to get the public's feelings. This campaign was continued for several years. In July 1884, the newspaper reported a rumor that the Donohoo building (Lot #77) on the corner of the public square was to be bought for a public school building and town hall. Ten years later, the old question of building a new city hall had been revived in the newspaper: "we trust the City Council will recognize the importance of the matter. It is an absolute necessity, and if we can't have such luxuries as decent sidewalks and electric lights, for goodness sake give us a respectable meeting house."

Ten years after this report, the trustees finally purchased a building on north Third on Lot #49. Ten years after that, they completed the remodeling of City Hall. The lower floor was the fire department, the upper front room was the council room, and the upper back room was the police court. A bell tower was added to the building.

On June 28, 1895, an editorial in the *Nelson County Record* read, "What the County Needs—Free Turnpikes, What the City Needs—Electric Lights, Water Works, City hall, Smooth Pavement, Decorous Street conduct, Riddance of Cows and Hogs, Health Regulations Enforced, Public Spirit. What the Citizens Need—An Ice Factory and some more factories."

This public request was answered in part by the trustees two months later with the purchase and erection of an electric light plant. The bid from General Electric Company of New York for $7,194 was accepted. These plans went back four years when the trustees established a fund of $5,000 toward an electric light plant and ice plant, provided that a like sum be raised by private subscription. At the same time, an additional fund of $5,000 toward building a town hall was promised. In March 1895, the choice was put to vote by the citizens. The election was held and 237 voted for and 15 against "Lighting city of Bardstown with Electricity."

In January 1896, the newspaper announced their approval of the new electric system:

Wednesday night for the first time, the twenty-five arc lights were turned on and the people generally happy. We failed to note a grumble on the part of anyone. The workmen seem to be getting along better lately, and are trying to please and satisfy all. The light also seems to be brighter, as was noticed particularly Wednesday night—perhaps on account of the extra pressure it was necessary to turn on account of the increase in the number of lights. Everyday new orders are entered and it will not be long before every residence in town will have them. When people become more accustomed to them they would not be without them; and property owners who desire to rent their houses, will be compelled to have same wired.

Four months later, they were printing details vindicating their campaign for an electric plant:

Where there is progress there is economy, likewise money.

It will be of interest to those who were so opposed to the establishing of an electric light plant here, on account of the increase of expense to

In 1884, it was suggested that the Donohoo building (behind the young men) be purchased for a public school building and town hall, using the first floor for the school rooms and tearing out all the partitions of the second and third stories to make a town hall. This proposal didn't happen.

the city to know that the income at present from private lights is almost sufficient to bring the cost of the street lamps down to that of the old coal-oil concerns. The income is now $120. Per month, and a sufficient number of others have subscribed to increase this amount to $150 per month. The running expenses of the plant amount to $2400 per year, $1800 deducted from $2400 leaves $600—the cost of the city lights. This is exactly what the coal-oil lamps cost exclusive of breakage.

On October 7, 1897, the council ordered that the light committee have the necessary lights put up to the courthouse for the October 11 reception of the Honorable William Jennings Bryan. Ten years before, when General Cassius M. Clay spoke at Bardstown, canvassing for the Republican nomination for governor, he had to be satisfied with coal-oil lamps.

Livestock running in the town streets was always a problem for the trustees. In the early years, laws were passed concerning the freedom of hogs, goats, and other animals, which were considered nuisances. In 1868, goats found running loose in town were ordered killed. In 1894, a compliment was published: "Main Street was thoroughly cleaned Monday. Marshal Warrell knows how to have the streets kept

This school was known as the Male and Female Institute when Professor Robert N. Cook was principal from 1896 to 1898. He is given credit for wiring the institute with electric lights in the summer of 1896. It was later known as the Bardstown Baptist Institute and was torn down in 1908.

clean, but we did see an awfully big hog on Main Street Tuesday. It surely must have been more than six months old."

Some years before, the town board had prohibited hogs from running free. The penalty was confiscation, selling, or killing of the hogs. The law was challenged by no less than the county judge when he wanted to be paid the value of his hogs that the city marshal had killed. The judge won and the law was revised. The *Nelson County Record* of June 28, 1895 reported, "At the last meeting of city dads, a hoss [*sic*] ordinance was passed to say nothing of a cow ordinance which wasn't passed, but the noble brute which are being so ruthlessly set aside by the bicycle still roams the streets unmolested, meditating over his troubles."

On August 19, 1898, the headlines on a column in the *Nelson County Record* read, "It Is Your Duty, Mr. Roby." Further headlines read, "To Make the Melon Wagons Vacate the Public Square—Abate the Nuisance." Melon wagons were congregating on the square and the filth from the horses, plus the decaying rinds of melons and other refuse, created a stench that could be scented a square away. It was likely to create sickness if not abated. All officials contacted disclaimed any jurisdiction in the matter, but investigation indicated that the county jailer was in charge of the public square. He was the superintendent of the square, courthouse, jail, stray pen, and other public county buildings at the seat of justice. The paper went on to request, "Now Mr. Roby, make the melon wagons remove to other localities, bring out some of the town prisoners and have them clean up the Square, and receive the thanks of the entire population of Bardstown for the service thus rendered."

In 1880, P.N. Pennebaker, deputy collector, and his posse made a raid on a moonshining distillery on the Bardstown-New Haven turnpike about 3 miles from New Haven. The still and 125 gallons of moonshine were destroyed; "[the] gentlemen who work by the pale silver light of the moon had left."

"Illicit distilling" was the proper name for the crime of making moonshine, which indicated that a person was not granted a permit by the government nor had he or she paid the tax on the product. In the Bardstown area in the last quarter of the nineteenth century, many licensed distillers produced whiskey known by the brand name around the country. Local barrel factories produced the containers, local farmers the grains, and Kentucky weather and water did the rest.

In the *Nelson County Record* in 1894, the following was reported:

> J.H. Beam Early Times is mashing 200 bushels—Haviland barrel factory working. Price & Thompson Distilleries near Manton in Washington county closed. "The Moonshine Distillery" owned by George N. Blanton & Co closed for season with a big blow-out at which a large number of people were present. The Moonshine is located near Deatsville.

In 1896, the magazine *The Nelson County Record, an Illustrated Historical and Industrial Supplement* was printed by Sam Carpenter Elliott. It included biographies of noted citizens and accounts of local distilleries. Elliott was a former revenue officer for the federal government and had worked at various operations in the area. Those distilleries that were operating in the county during this period produced nationally recognized brands.

In the southern part of Nelson County, along the Knoxville branch of the L&N Railroad, were located several distilleries. The Belle of Nelson Distillery was located at New Hope. Local horseman John Mattingly ran a filly named Belle of Nelson in the Kentucky Oaks horse race the day before the Kentucky Derby in the 1870s. After she won, her name was used for a whiskey and a distillery. It was first produced by Mattingly and Moore Distillery. Later, the label was sold to the New Hope Distillery of the same name.

The E.L. Miles Distillery and New Hope Distillery were located in New Hope. Miles Distillery was established in 1796 by Henry Miles and was in continuous operation except for three years during the Civil War. The New Hope Distillery was established in 1875, and was operated by Edward Miles and Thomas H. Sherley. E.L. Miles and New Hope were the brands.

Several other distilleries operated during this time. Cold Spring was operated by J. Bernard Dant and Crittenden Clark at Gethsemane Station. Nelson County Club pure rye and Cold Spring were the brands. Nelson County Distillery Company was located at Coon Hollow. Two distilleries were operated: Coon Hollow and Big Spring. On November 17, 1884 the Coon Hollow Distillery was burned by an arsonist with a loss of 1,491 barrels of whiskey. Coon Hollow and Big Spring were also the names of the brands. Willow Springs was a few hundred yards from Coon Hollow Station. Although it was owned by both P. Cummins and Martin J. Cummins, it was operated by Martin. Willow Springs and Minway Club were the brands. Located on the Springfield branch of the L&N Railroad was the S.P. Lancaster Distillery. Named for the distiller, S.P. Lancaster, it was the only brand made since 1850. Also on the same railroad line, but closer to Bardstown, was the Early Times Distillery. It was owned by B.H. Hurt and John H. Beam. Beam believed in the early methods of making whiskey—mashing the grains in small tubs and boiling the beer and whiskey in copper stills over open fires. Early Times, A.G. Nall, and Jack Beam were the brands.

Traveling west from Bardstown along the Bardstown branch line of the L&N Railroad there were several distilleries. The Beam and Hart Distillery was located about 2 miles northwest of town. David M. Beam began the distillery in 1853. He retired in 1892 and transferred the business to his son James B. Beam and son-in-law Albert Hart. Old Tub was the only brand. Gwynn Spring Distillery was listed at Hunters Depot. It was established in the 1870s by Jefferson D. McGee and a Mr. Walker. It was rebuilt after burning in 1880. John B. Stoner was in partnership with a Mr. McGee. W.B. Samuels and Company Distillery was located at Samuels. The distillery was established in 1869 by Samuels, who then entered into partnership with George R. Burkes. W.B. Samuels Bourbon and Eureka Rye were the brands. A half-mile east of the railroad at Deatsville was the Taylor W. Samuels Distillery, erected by T.W. Samuels in 1844 and continuously operated by him.

This view is of Roseland Academy after it was purchased by James B. Beam in 1909. He remodeled it for a residence and added the porch. Beam and his father were both distillers. He is sitting at far left, with his father D.M.Beam at the far right.

T.W. Samuels is the only brand. Murphy, Barber and Company was located at Clermont. The fountainhead of the springs, which supply the water for whiskey-making, is located in Nelson County, so one can claim them as a local distillery. In 1881, Squire Murphy, A.M. Barber, and Calvin Brown established this distillery. Murphy, Barber and Company and Clermont Rye were the brands.

On the west edge of Bardstown on College (now Withrow) Creek, was the F.G. Walker Distillery. Established by Walker in 1881, it was soon operated by his partner, Charles C. Brown. F.G. Walker and Queen of Nelson were the brands.

The next four distilleries were south of Bardstown on the Bardstown-Green River Turnpike. The Mattingly and Moore Distillery was a half-mile southwest of the courthouse. Established in 1876, it used the never-failing Morton Spring for the limestone spring water necessary for good whiskey. John Simms and R.H. Edlen were the owners. Simms Edelen was the brand. Just a little farther down the road was the Tom Moore Distillery. It was established in 1889 by Thomas S. Moore, following his management of the Mattingly and Moore Distillery until 1889. Tom Moore and Woodcock were the brands. The Henry Sutherland Distillery was established by William Sutherland in 1824 and operated by his son after his death in 1862. Old Sutherland was the brand name. Almost to New Haven was the Ford Brothers Distilleries. R. Monroe Ford was the president and

After the controversy over the extension of the railroad to Springfield in 1886, this long metal and wood trestle was constructed over the Bloomfield pike from the Bardstown depot to the Wickland farm. It still stands in the twenty-first century.

general manager with his brothers Thomas R. and Curtis J. as silent members. The distiller was Richard Bowling, who was "a believer in signs as displayed by the moon. When he is making whiskey in the dark of the moon he always exceeds 4 gallons per bushel, while in the light of the moon he can only produce about 4 gallons per bushel."

Another operation off the beaten path was the Walnut Hollow Distillery near Howardstown. It was first established by Fred Bray in 1831, but James Mahoney, father of the present owner, operated it until 1888, when he entered into a partnership with Miles A. Howard. In 1895, James H. Mahoney bought Howard's interest and became the sole owner. Walnut Hollow is the brand.

Though not Nelson County distilleries, J.M. Atherton Distilleries shipped its whiskey from the New Haven Depot in Nelson County. Located right across the Rolling Fork River in Larue County, it began manufacturing in 1867 on the present site of the Mayfield House. The Atherton Distillery was the other, larger operation. Old Johnnie Boone, whose father Wattie was probably the oldest distiller in Kentucky, made whiskey here for years. It was at this location that Thomas Lincoln worked for Boone's Distillery. Peter Lee Atherton, the son of the owner, was in charge of the distillery plant. Atherton, Mayfield, Clifton, Windsor, Howard, Carter, Kenwood, Brownfield, and Baker were the brands.

Going to the northeast edge of Nelson County, two distilleries were located away from the others. The McKenna Distillery was located in Fairfield. Henry McKenna began the operation in 1855 with a flour mill. He made less than one barrel of whiskey a day. In 1883, he built a new brick distillery and increased production to three barrels a day. He died in 1893, leaving his sons Daniel McKenna, James S. McKenna, and Stafford McKenna to continue the business. H. McKenna, Old Line, and Handmade Sour Mash Whiskey were the brands.

Just down the road at Bloomfield was the Sugar Valley Distillery in the suburbs of the town. Bodine and Samuel McClaskey purchased it from David Brooks in 1889.

These 24 distilleries would shrink to 12 by the time of Prohibition in 1920, but the brands they began continued to be bottled and sold through the next 100 years.

In the spring of 1882, there was a general move to seek construction of a railroad between Bardstown and Springfield. Four years later, this extension of the Bardstown Branch was liberally funded by local distillers, merchants, and farmers. Nevertheless, in November, a controversy about the possibility of a route chosen to bypass the town itself and branch off before the end of the line brought outcries of rage. The owners of the land to be crossed from the town depot toward Springfield were requesting more money for the use of the right-of-way than the railroad company wanted to pay. Lawsuits were filed, but were dismissed so that the railroad could determine if a relocation of the line north of Bardstown—leaving the main line at the Nazareth trestle and running across the lands of Pen Talbott, John Talbott, John S. Humphreys, William Johnson, J.B. McGinnis, Joseph Hart, Meb. Magruder, Beverly Grigsby and others—would form a junction with the line already located from J.H. Beam's to Springfield. The railroad company claimed it would shorten the line 2 to 4 miles. It was thought that the northern route would be more expensive. The final decision placed the extension of the railroad from the end of the tracks at the depot to the designed plan at J.H. Beam's.

In the 1890s, the turnpikes built and operated by private companies for the last 50 years were being taken over by the government. Many complaints about the condition of the roads, some being impassable at times, pushed the state government to act. A state survey of roads in May 1895 determined that Nelson County had 200 to 300 miles of pike roads in good condition with a net revenue of $8,835. The general assembly passed a free turnpike bill in 1896 to raise taxes to purchase the turnpikes. This decision was so unpopular that violence broke out in many areas of Kentucky. Burning or dynamiting of tollgates, and other damage to the roads, pressured the toll companies to sell the roads to the counties who operated them without tolls.

The sinking of the battleship *Maine* in Havana Harbor in the spring of 1898 created a feeling of nationalism and the Kentucky State Guard volunteered their services. The local unit, the Nelson Rifles, were notified of a call into service on April 2, 1898. Company C of Third Regiment, with Lieutenant L.E. McKay as commander, received orders from Colonel T.J. Smith of Bowling Green for the Third Regiment of the Kentucky State Guard to assemble.

There were 80 men enrolled, but they needed 103 for a full complement. Captain D.Y. Beckham, studying law in Baltimore, would rejoin his company.

There was a subscription started to raise funds for a flag for the company. Material was purchased and some women made a very handsome flag. Company C would be assigned to the Battalion of the First Regiment. The War Department called for two troops of cavalry and three regiments of infantry from Kentucky.

In late April, Company C still lacked about 10 men of their full complement. Captain Beckham had arrived and they were awaiting orders to move to Lexington for a ten-day drill. Many had joined from the country without funds to sustain themselves while awaiting the call and a public subscription was made to help out. A handsome silk flag, 6 feet by 6 feet, 6 inches, was formally presented by Miss Carrie Crosby. The unit was now comprised of 59 privates, 1 wagoner, 1 artiller, 12 corporals, 4 sergeants, 1 quartermaster, 1 orderly, 2 musicians, 2 lieutenants, and 1 captain for a total of 84. They had received orders to remove south, but first, on May 6, 1898, the Nelson Rifles received orders to go into camp at Lexington.

A report of the conditions at Lexington for the local boys did not give rest to the idea they were undergoing hardships. Company C was housed in a small barn with 3 other companies making up 320 men. There was a great lack of beds and bedding, and the straw was beginning to smell. The soldiers' smoking was a constant danger. The men were encouraged by the fact that their officers were bunking with them in the loft, not like other companies. Their fare was ill-cooked and insufficient. Physical examinations of the troops began, and it was reported that 17 of Company C were rejected because of physical defects and would return in Bardstown soon.

On the homefront, entertainment was held for the benefit of the Nelson Rifles. The admissions and donations totaled $29, which was sent to Lexington. On May 31, the Nelson Rifles were ordered to the Chickamauga encampment in Georgia. They were transported on a special train, arriving on June 3. A report noted that they remained in the cars all night:

> Wagons were sent to transport us to the Park. We loaded the baggage and the sick members placed aboard, started for camp. We received our tents in the evening and the boys began to build their houses. The tents are crowded with six to a tent. Most of the water has to be carried one half a mile. Company C. drills five hours every day and is doing better than the majority of the companies in the Third Regiment. We will be equipped either Monday or Tuesday.
>
> Our eating is composed of beans, bacon, coffee and hard tack for ten days and then we get much better. We also get potatoes.

Captain Beckham wrote to the Bardstown City Council asking for a donation toward a regimental flag. He noted that other towns in the area had contributed. The council agreed and donated $25. On July 1, the Third Regiment was ordered to Cuba, but illness struck these soldiers, officers, and privates alike. The Third Kentucky, under the command of Colonel Smith, loaded on the afternoon of July

27 and left Chattanooga for Newport News. There they expected to board a ship for Cuba, but measles, mumps, and other illness bumped the Third Regiment from the ship at Newport News. The Spanish surrendered and the Third Regiment left for Lexington on their way home.

The Nelson County Record *reported the first casualty of the war with Spain on July 26: "Sergeant George Lancaster Smith (on the right), gallant member of company C died in the camp hospital at Chickamauga, last Sunday after a brief illness of typhoid fever." The others are Muir McGill and John Hurst.*

5. Beginning of the Twentieth Century, 1900–1920

Bardstown was growing; new utilities, public buildings, and public schools were needed. Celebrations were held for Saint Joseph Cathedral's 100th anniversary, the "Great War" soldiers returned, and Saint Joseph College reopened. A time of mourning was experienced after the worst disaster to hit Bardstown, the Shepherdsville Train Wreck. On February 3, 1900, Lieutenant Governor John Crepps Wickliffe Beckham, native of Bardstown, was sworn in as governor after the assassination of Governor William Goebels. Nine months later at a special election, he won by less than 1 percent of the vote.

Now that Bardstown had electric lights, the public wanted running water. Up until that point, cisterns and wells were used for public water and fire protection. In 1903, the majority voted that Bardstown should have a system of waterworks. The reservoir was created by damming Barber's Hollow on Town Creek. The resulting lake contained approximately 29 million gallons, enough to supply the city for a period of nine months. Passing through an aerator, then filtered through sand, gravel, and beaten rock, the water was pumped by two pumps with enough pressure to "throw water twice as high as any building in the town." The system was estimated to cost $22,500, which included 30 fire hydrants. "In five years the town paid the electric light plant debt of $7500 and interest" without raising taxation on property. Not one citizen expressed himself against the proposition.

The city council was concerned over the cost of the electric light system in the fall of 1905. Investigation showed that people were leaving their lights on all night—three times more than other communities. "The register at the power house shows that over 500 sixteen candle power lights are kept turned on all night, that is an average of ten hours of the twenty-four. It was never intended when the rates were established that the lights would be kept burning all night." (Rates were based on the number of light bulbs in a building.) After comparing the cost of the coal that was used to generate electricity at the power plant, and how much money could be saved, which could be used to pave all the streets, the new night rate ordinance was in the best interests of the city.

Bardstown's 20-year-old telephone service was in jeopardy. In 1906, a controversy broke out between the Bardstown City Council and the Cumberland

This 1905 view of Third Street looking north from court square still shows the poles and wires of the Cumberland Telephone. and Telegraph Company. They were ordered removed after the company lost the city franchise.

Telephone and Telegraph Company over the right to run their lines and poles on the street right-of-way in town. The telephone company announced in December 1905 that rates would go up 65¢ per customer. They claimed that, for the "better (long distance) service which they supplied," they needed to charge more. After an investigation and comparison, the council determined that Bardstown customers were not getting equal service for the charges. A proposed increase of 25¢ per phone was not accepted by the telephone company. When the council discovered that the telephone company did not have a contract to use the street right-of-ways, a franchise for telephone service was advertised for bid. Cumberland refused to bid on it and it was bought by two unnamed local men, who proposed to run an independent system. The council told the public that the poles and wires of the Cumberland T&T would be removed and the new service installed as soon as possible. An accommodation was worked out and one improvement out of this fray was the removal of poles from Third Street.

At the beginning of the twentieth century in Bardstown, a higher level of education could be obtained from the private schools: Nazareth Academy, Nelson Normal School, Bardstown Baptist Institute, and Saint Monica's. The desire of the community fathers to provide education for all children resulted in the

117

organization of new schools and construction of new buildings in the first decade of the new century.

"The cornerstone of the new colored public school building will be laid on July 7, 1903. A grand street parade, headed by a brass band, a chorus of 200 children, orator and music will be features of the occasion," reported *The Kentucky Standard* of April 30, 1903. This school was known as the "Bluff School" and operated until 1923 when the Nelson County Training School was constructed across the street. The Bardstown Graded School building was erected in 1908 at a cost of $30,000. Principal Ernest Fulton would oversee the teachers and students. A high school building was added in 1927. These new public schools resulted in lower enrollment at the private schools, causing the closing of Nelson Normal School and Bardstown Baptist Institute. By 1910, "old Bethlehem Academy" proposed to build a brick addition in the place of a frame building on the north side of the school. By this time, the enrollment at Bardstown Graded School was 190, Nazareth Academy was 125, and Bethlehem Academy was 105.

On October 7, 1915, Nelson County School Superintendent W.T. McClain announced in an article that "the Moonlight school supplies have arrived, First Readers, tablets, pencils, etc. They can be had by calling at my office." Nelson County's illiterate adults were going to neighborhood one-room schools to learn to read and write. Schools were operated between 7 p.m. and 9 p.m. on the first four nights of the week by volunteer teachers at their schools. Since moonlight

This is the 1910 brick addition replacing a frame building on the north side of old Bethlehem Academy. "Large classrooms, music rooms and an auditorium will occupy the ground floor and first story while play rooms and lunch rooms will be fitted up in the basement."

Built in 1908 of brick and stone, Bardstown Graded School offered eight lower grades and four full years of high school. "Every boy and girl in Nelson County, who can give sufficient proof that he or she are prepared to take the high school course is entitled to free tuition."

was needed in order to travel to the schools after dark, they became known as "moonlight schools." The Kentucky Illiteracy Commission furnished instruction and equipment. Cora Wilson Stewart began this movement in eastern Kentucky. After it spread to the west, she issued a competitive challenge to the two regions to teach those who had missed early schooling. During the summer months, volunteers from larger schools or colleges came to the county and organized the schools.

In Nelson County by 1918, schools in Boston, Botland, Samuels, Balltown, and Russell Schoolhouse all reported on their night classes. The teachers did not receive any additional pay for the night classes, only the satisfaction of teaching these adults the skills they missed learning in their youth.

McClain's position was challenged by local teacher Mary L. Wood on August 2, 1917. She did not win, but it gave women the chance to vote for a woman. Five years before this election, it was publicized that, for the first time in Kentucky's history, women would be able to cast a vote to elect their choice in the subdistrict school trustees and the county superintendent races. All women who were over 21 years of age, who could read and write, and who had resided in the district for 60 days, were eligible to vote. Any woman meeting those conditions with signatures from five residents would also be eligible to hold office.

The Xaverian Brothers purchased the old Saint Joseph College buildings in 1911. On September 14, they had a formal reopening of the college at 8:00. "Nearly 1500 persons had gathered on the college campus to hear the speakers." The buildings needed extensive remodeling after the Saint Thomas Orphanage

In 1911, Apostolic delegate Reverend Diomede Falconio came to the formal reopening ceremonies of Saint Joseph College. A motorcade led by the marching Knights of Columbus from the depot to the cathedral passed many people eager to view the visitors. He is being greeted by Father C.J. O'Connell.

vacated them in the fall of 1910. Local architect and contractor E.B. Smith, working with E.G. Wooten, supervised the installation of lighting, heating, and sanitation equipment. The razing of the oldest section, the left wing or "L," and the transformation of the second story of the right wing into a chapel were the biggest changes. Flaget Hall was put in "perfect repair" and contained classrooms and a study hall. In the main building were the dormitories, refectories (dining rooms), and private rooms for the faculty and boarding students.

The school opened with 70 pupils on September 14. Immediately, sports programs became newsworthy. Articles in *The Kentucky Standard* noted "Football revives in Bardstown." For the next few years, the newspaper reported basketball, track (or "running teams"), baseball, debate, and chess clubs competing against local and Louisville teams. Three years after reopening, the following was reported:

> The college crack [*sic*] team which was organized three weeks ago is doing good work . . . the boys always accompanied by one of the Brothers, take long distance walks, sometimes they run part of the way. . . . Two weeks ago, the distance from Balltown six miles from here and the return trip twelve miles in all, was made by the lads in two and a half hours.

120

The cornerstone of the First Cathedral in the Bardstown diocese was laid on July 16, 1816. One hundred years later, the community observed its anniversary with a week-long celebration. "On Sunday July 16, Bishop Flaget Day, Abbot Obrecht of Gethsemani Abbey and Most Reverend J.J. Glennon, Archbishop of St. Louis, Mo. will participate in the High Mass at 10:00." On Thursday, Bishop D. O'Donaghue, bishop of Louisville, blessed the Centennial Memorial Monument. This was unveiled by Edwin Mann, the great-great-grandson of John Rogers, the architect-builder of the cathedral. It was reported that 1,500 people were present for the unveiling and ceremonies. Eight hundred people were seated inside on the pews with additional chairs and benches placed in the aisles. Three hundred people remained on the church lawn during the services and at least three hundred people returned home.

Father C.J. O'Connell was recognized for his care of the cathedral. In his renovation of the building in the early years of his pastorage, he employed Max Leber in 1882 to fresco the whitewashed interior of the church and he had just had it repainted by Leber's son Guy in preparation for the centennial celebration. The article about this occasion noted the claim about the "priceless" paintings. It named all the famous painters and the value of the collection at more than $1 million. This article and others reported in the Louisville papers began the controversy about the origin of the paintings and their value.

Historians, local and national, began to doubt the local claims of Louis Phillipe living here, teaching school, and being the donor of the artworks. Publications and articles for both sides of the claims continued for the next 10 years, with no one "backing up."

For World War I, there were 1,899 Nelson County men between 18 and 46 years of age registered for military service by September 18, 1918. More than 800 local men served in this conflict. The list of soldiers and their units was compiled by county historian Ludwell McKay in a book immediately after the war. A local U.S. Boy's Working Reserve was organized with boys between ages 16 and 21 to assist in harvesting crops or other aids to the war effort.

Letters from various servicemen about camp life and experiences were printed in the paper. In January 1918, there was a local shortage of coal. Because of the shortage of fuel for the electric generators, a call for conservation of electricity was issued. People began using wood again to heat and cook, and they used kerosene to illuminate. "Tagging Shovels" was a project taken on by the younger people to tie a string or ribbon on every coal shovel in the schools and homes to remind people to use coal sparingly. Local distilleries advertised for young women to work in the bottling houses due to the shortage of men.

A Nelson County Red Cross chapter was organized. Meeting at workrooms in their communities for a "Spend Day" of sewing and knitting, patriotic women knitted socks, wool helmets, mufflers, and sweaters. They sewed shirts, wash rags, handkerchiefs, napkins, and tray covers. "Old Fashioned Basket Dinner and Patriotic Meeting" was a full-page ad for the benefit of the Red Cross activities and war stamp sales, and was paid for by local businesses.

Most of the local recruits were sent to Camp Taylor in Louisville where, in the fall of 1918, an epidemic of Spanish Influenza was reported. It had spread across the United States and, on October 10, the local health department issued an emergency order from the surgeon general closing all schools, places of amusement, churches, and other places of assembly. The local phone company apologized because so many of their operators were sick, they could not handle all the traffic. *The Kentucky Standard*'s work force was sick and the newspaper was late. Although physicians advised persons having influenza not to drink alcohol, there are those who believed to the contrary, and authorities were considering lifting the ban on liquor so that it could be brought into local option territory. The ban was lifted on schools and churches, and the schools reopened on November 11, the same day Germany surrendered. The ban was reinstated in early December when illness again broke out in the schools. By December 24, 24 people had died from the flu. No list of the number who got sick but survived was noted, but later issues of the newspaper show people who succumbed from other illnesses after they had been weakened by the flu. McKay's list of casualties in May 1919 indicated that 31 soldiers died, 15 by disease.

On August 6, 1919, the soldiers' memorial was unveiled at Saint Joseph. The monument of bronze figures of victory and liberty on native coral stone was erected to remember the men who served in the great war and those who gave their lives: Joseph Raoul Losson, Chester Stewart, W. Tom Rapier, and Herman Evans. It was also the occasion of the tenth anniversary of the consecration of the

This was the first memorial in the United States to be dedicated to the memory of soldiers in World War I. It was erected in front of the church on the 100th anniversary of Saint Joseph Cathedral's consecration on August 8, 1919.

This turn-of-the-century view of Saint Joseph Church doesn't disclose its age. The congregation celebrated 100 years on August 8, 1919 with a dedication of a war memorial to the soldiers of the parish who died in World War I.

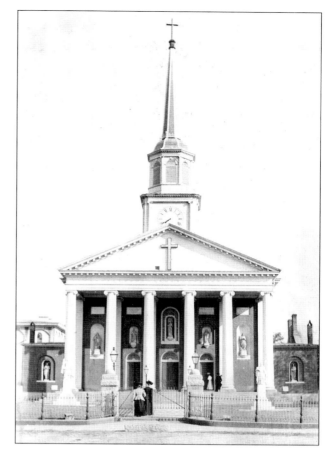

cathedral. Less than a year later, on April 8, 1920, Reverend C.J. O'Connell died after a long illness, leaving old Saint Joseph Church as his monument.

December 20, 1917 was a snowy Thursday afternoon. A rush of warmly clad shoppers: gentlemen, ladies, children, servants of all ages, many of them family groups, hurried down the Louisville streets to board the train for Bardstown and points southeast.

Mrs. Joseph Hurst had taken her infant son Raoul into Louisville to consult a specialist about his health. She was accompanied by an African-American nurse, Annie Reed. Ben Talbott, a deputy United States Internal Revenue collector, was attending tax school with James Thompson, also of the Revenue department. They hurried to catch the *Accommodation*. As the time neared for departure, Mr. and Mrs. John Phillips and their daughter Ella left their other daughter Mae at the hospital. Redford Cherry, county attorney, and his wife and son met at the station. Little Redford Jr. was excited about his trip to see Santa Claus. Many of these passengers carried the Christmas gifts they had traveled to Louisville that morning to obtain.

The train, loaded with more than 100 people, left the station a few minutes behind schedule. Due at Shepherdsville at 5:19 p.m., it arrived about six minutes late. The telegraph operator, aware that the Cincinnati and New Orleans Flyer No. 7 was running three hours late and due to arrive, asked the dispatcher what arrangements to make. The answer was, "arrange a passing at this station." He gave orders to the *Accommodation* to take the siding. The four cars and engine pulled up about 200 feet past the siding, prepared to back off the main track. The signal was set against the fast train, but the roar of the approaching train was clearly heard. The telegraph operator grabbed a red lantern and ran out to signal frantically. The 20 passengers who had just left the cars watched in horror as they realized that they were to witness the terrible fate of their traveling companions. The faster train, made up of the heavy engine, several baggage cars, and passenger coaches, all of steel construction, plowed into the wooden passenger cars of the *Accommodation*. The two rear passenger cars were splintered into fragments and shattered bodies. The impact threw people out into the snowdrifts, the cars were pushed over the sides of the tracks, and, 150 feet after the impact, the mass of wreckage was halted.

Stunned by what they had seen, the people of Shepherdsville immediately began to render aid. The L&N office was notified and a relief train was organized from Louisville. At 6:45 p.m., the special train left Union Station with surgeons, physicians, and nurses. Meanwhile, the shocked and injured were taken to the nearby depot and church. Some of the passengers were able to extract themselves only to expire. Those discovered dead in the wreckage appeared to have been snapped back by the impact, suffering fatal head injuries.

The special train provided trained medical care and transportation back to Louisville. Saints Mary and Elizabeth Hospital had been alerted to the arrival of the victims. The Louisville police department arranged policemen and vehicles to help transport patients from the depot to the hospital. The Army Ambulance Corps from Camp Taylor sent 100 men, doctors, and interns, plus 30 ambulances to the station to assist.

Meanwhile, in Bardstown, the first news came from the depot at New Haven and spread throughout the community. Those who knew of friends and relatives on the train prayed for a telephone call or a telegram of reassurance. As the rumors of the tragedy increased, some members of the community sped to the Shepherdsville site, while others, including doctors, went directly to the Louisville hospital.

The first real news of the dead and seriously injured was received from the *Courier Journal* reports early in the night. The railroad had admitted earlier that between 40 and 50 people were dead, but hope was still alive that not all of the Bardstown people had perished. The Sisters of Charity at Saints Mary and Elizabeth Hospital were praying at the altar at the hospital as they awaited the relief train. When they heard the train whistle, they arose to render what comfort they could to the injured and sorrowing. Joseph Muir obtained the news of his brother's death in the wreck at the hospital. His sister-in-law died as she was borne into the building. His nephew also died. The relatives of Mrs. Tom Moore, accompanied by Dr. Grigsby, were met with the sad tidings of her death. On and on, the sorrows multiplied. As the first papers were distributed, the impact of this, the worst wreck in the history of the L&N Railroad, became known throughout the country. Telegrams from California, Florida, Texas, and many other states arrived at the office in Bardstown.

On December 21, 1917, a special train left the Tenth Street Station in Louisville at 3:00. Carrying the bodies of 23 victims of the railroad wreck, it would finish the journey that these poor souls began 24 hours before. Eighteen bodies were taken to Bardstown where they were received by a town in mourning. People had been waiting an hour or more for the bodies, which were carried in a baggage car, the coffins strewn with flowers. As they were taken up the street, mourners could be seen walking alongside saying the rosary. Another three of the victims were taken to Springfield and two were delivered at the Samuels Station. Twelve other victims remained at Shepherdsville.

The city of Bardstown was numb with grief. All businesses were closed, except for the necessities of life. The council and mayor issued an unnecessary appeal to forego the usual festivities of the Christmas season. All bells were tolling and flags

This photo, taken the morning after the train wreck, shows the complete destruction of the wooden rail cars. This view is of the wreckage-strewn track and splintered remains of the wooden passenger cars, illustrating the force of the crash and the miracle of those who survived.

drooped at half-mast. Bardstown mourned. In total, 54 people were killed by the Shepherdsville train wreck, considered by many as the most traumatic event of Bardstown's and Nelson County's history.

In the summer of 1992, original photographs of this train wreck were discovered in evidence folders in the Nelson Circuit Court records. They were used in the lawsuits instigated by the injured and heirs of the deceased. Of the multitude of lawsuits that grew out of the wreck, only one went to trial, and the L&N Railroad settled with the injured and the heirs of the deceased.

Two photographers of Louisville, Bramson and Piers, took a total of twelve 8-inch by 10-inch photographs, some of which were published in the newspapers at the time. These views are of the wreckage-strewn track and the splintered remains of the wooden passenger cars. They illustrated the force of the crash and the miracle of those who survived better than any written account.

December 20th, 1917 was a snowy Thursday afternoon. Bardstown families had taken the train to Louisville to shop for the holidays. This was the end of their trip when their cars were rammed from behind by a heavier train.

6. ECONOMIC SHUTDOWN, 1920–1940

During Prohibition, tourism was sought to replace the liquor industry. The purchase of My Old Kentucky Home as a state park, the erection of the John Fitch Monument, and the promotion of the community for visiting was a new industry. Bardstown was aided by the repeal of Prohibition in 1933 because legal whiskey-making then returned.

The dreaded day was here. No legal liquor sales. No production at the distilleries. In January 1920, the law-abiding attitude of many Nelson Countians changed forever. At the 12 or so distilleries, an effort to market the stored spirits before the ban lowered some inventory, but many barrels resided in the warehouses. (In March 1924, there were an estimated 600,000 gallons of whiskey in Nelson County.) Many distilleries had been sold; all had been shut down. Mattingly and Moore at Bardstown was bankrupt. Athertonville in nearby LaRue County was being dismantled. Clear Spring near Nazareth, Dant near Gethsemane, F.G. Walker, and H. Sutherland outside of Bardstown were auctioned in 1918. The local saloons closed. Everyone was stocking up on spirits, not knowing when they could legally obtain them again, but Nelson Countians did not let the law halt their age-old tradition of turning corn into comfort—or of sharing that comfort with others—for a price of course.

"Prohibition enforcement officers made a sweeping crusade against bootleggers and their ilk, in and leaving Nelson County during the latter part of last week. Sixteen 'leggers,' five alleged moonshiners, thirteen automobiles and one illicit still was part of the lot obtained by the officials," read the May 25, 1922 newspaper. This was one of the many accounts of the capture of "transporters," or those who moved moonshine or illegal whiskey to the bigger cities from the hills of Nelson and Marion Counties.

One of the favorite spots for officials to set up a road block was the covered bridge over the Beech Fork River south of Bardstown. Cars and trucks coming from New Haven, Balltown, New Hope, and points south were stopped and searched. Some of these vehicles had been specially fitted with tanks and hidden reservoirs to haul moonshine.

Exciting chases up and down the hills and curves of Nelson County captured many bootleggers going to Louisville and "the big city market." Most of these "white mule runners" were out-of-county crooks who gambled they could outrun or outwit country lawmen. But the United States officials patrolled the roads and streets leading through Bardstown, particularly one known to them as "Alcohol Avenue." On one occasion, when 200 gallons of "moon" was discovered in a Ford on this street, it was poured into the ditch in front of Saint Joseph College and ignited.

When transporters or moonshiners were arrested, their vehicles and stills were confiscated. When these vehicles were sold at auction, they were occasionally purchased by other transporters. The stills were destroyed on the spot. Destroying the whiskey could be a hazard. Two Prohibition officers were badly burned when a whiskey barrel exploded as they poured it on their smoldering fire. Most of the time, the whiskey and mash was dumped into the nearest waterway.

Warehouse robberies were another story. Thieves siphoned whiskey from the barrels with a hose and replaced it with water. They hauled it away in metal milk cans or just stole the barrels outright. Some distilleries would be hit multiple times in a few months.

The raids on reported stills were lively affairs with shotguns and pistols being waved and discharged. In the July 14, 1921 newspaper, a highly emotional report noted that shots from an ambush wounded two officers and ignited public furor. A "posse" of more than 100 "prominent business and professional men" from Bardstown was deputized to chase down the ambushers in the Mill Creek and Bear Creek areas. Two groups of men searched the two areas. The Bear Creek posse uncovered five stills and wounded three "unidentified" moonshiners on Bear Creek. It was unclear if they were the ambushers.

Everyone got in on the chase as four Boy Scouts rafting down the Beech Fork heard singing and smelled an odor that one called "like Ma cooking biscuits." They told their parents and local officials, who then discovered a still and moonshiners. The confiscation of "an excellent Cadilac [sic], $100.00 fine, and 30 days in jail" was imposed on two men, who plead guilty to transporting whiskey after 90 gallons of moonshine was discovered in their car.

On July 4, 1923, a steady stream of traffic came into Bardstown from all directions. A special train from Louisville carrying 441 people arrived at the depot. Fifteen thousand people gathered to dedicate the house that inspired Stephen C. Foster to write his famous song, "My Old Kentucky Home." Anticipating the traffic, a select squad of 12 men on motorcycles was sent from the Louisville police force to handle the estimated 6,000 cars that day. These diligent officers embarrassed Mayor John Sisco—he was stopped for speeding to the festivities.

The natural amphitheater at the front of the house was covered with people, who enjoyed Foster melodies and patriotic airs played by the 10th Infantry Band from Camp Knox. Arch H. Pulliam, vice-chairman of the Old Kentucky Home Commission, presented the site to the state. Governor Edwin P. Morrow accepted the home as one of Kentucky's treasures. This event was the culmination of three years of planning and promotion, and was the first of many such entertaining affairs at the "home."

This is the front parlor of Federal Hill when it was purchased by the Old Kentucky Home Commission in 1922. Souvenirs of Mrs. Frost's travels were displayed with her family furniture. The fireplaces were used to heat the home.

Judge Osso Stanley approached Mrs. Madge Rowan Frost, the granddaughter of original builder John Rowan, in 1920 about the possibility of purchasing the Rowan farm for a historic park. Visited by many locals and their guests over the years, it was acknowledged as Foster's inspiration. A $50,000 purchase price was agreed upon and a $7,000 option was paid in the fall of 1920.

Governor Edwin Morrow appointed four people from each political party to the Old Kentucky Home Commission. They kicked off a campaign in March 1921 whose slogan, "My Old Kentucky Home Let's Buy it. Does it Touch Your Heart, Let it Touch your Pocketbook," brought forth an outpouring of funds from successful Kentuckians in other states, as well as pennies from schoolchildren around the commonwealth. Nelson County's contribution was $12,000 and this was raised by local events such as baseball games between local teams, "Has Beens and the Down & Outs."

In August, the commission reported that fundraising efforts had produced $60,800. They still needed $10,000 to construct a road, erect a tablet about the park, and make the necessary repairs to the house. The state legislature approved a $20,000 donation and yearly funding at the next session in January 1922. The vote was punctuated with the singing of the song led by the legislators. (It was officially adopted as the state song in 1928.) With this pledge in hand, plans

On May 25,1927, 1,000 people gathered for the unveiling of the John Fitch Monument. This view is from the east side of the courthouse. It shows the flag being pulled away from in front of the monument. In the background is the first water tower in Bardstown on Second Street. The four-story Hite-Donohoo-Boone building on the right was demolished six months later for an automobile agency.

continued, and work began to repaint and re-paper the inside of the home. A terrible wind and rain storm in the spring of 1923 damaged the roof and set back the construction, but repairs were completed for the opening on July 4.

The commission employed Colonel Ben LaBree, ex-Confederate soldier, historian, and author to be the first curator. His grandiose tales about the Rowan family, the construction of the house with "English brick brought over the mountains by ox carts," and glorified southern life continues to confuse historians delving into the Federal Hill story.

Royalty came to Bardstown on November 18, 1926 when Queen Marie of Rumania and her party arrived in a convoy of touring cars. Congressman Ben Johnson was chairman of the Governor's Committee and escorted Her Highness. The party left Louisville at 11:30 for Bardstown, speeding at an average of 45 miles per hour and led by two motorcycle policemen. Crowds of people lined the streets of Bardstown and greeted them as they drove to Federal Hill.

The dining room table at My Old Kentucky Home was set with the Johnson family china and decorated with flags of the United States and Rumania. Tables were set up in other rooms to accommodate all of the party. After the ceremonies and a luncheon, the 15-car entourage paid a short visit to Saint Joseph Cathedral, then raced off to Hodgenville and the Lincoln Birthplace Memorial. Dust flew from the roads as this parade set speed records averaging 60 miles per hour! Uphill and down, speeding cars slid into ditches, overheated, and threw bearings. Both motorcycles were disabled, leaving the queen's car to proceed with only the national flags flying to denote the importance of this visitor.

On May 25, 1927, 1,000 people gathered on the court square in Bardstown to hear Governor W.J. Fields state, "History has taught us, the textbooks in our schools have taught our children, that Robert Fulton was the inventor of the steamboat and the public accepted that teaching as true." He went on to say, "Yes, a few people knew that it was not true," as he recognized the efforts of Mrs. Ben Johnson and the John Fitch Chapter of the Daughters of the American Revolution to honor the real inventor of the steamboat, John Fitch. Colonel J.R.R. Hannay of the War Department presented the $15,000 monument to the care of the Fitch Chapter DAR. The memorial was accepted by Mrs. Ben Johnson, speaking as regent for and on behalf of the local chapter. An American flag was silently moved to the side by guy-ropes pulled by Miss Anne Talbott, granddaughter of Mrs. Johnson. Misses Charlotte and Frances Fitch, descendants of John Fitch, stood at either side. Former Congressman Ben Johnson gave an interesting summary of the history of Fitch's invention and the efforts to obtain congressional recognition, plus the necessary appropriation needed to build the monument. Five members of Fitch's family attended the ceremony.

The article noted that Charles Fitch, great-great-grandson of John Fitch, stated that "he had looked forward to a day such as this for fifty years. As a boy he knew that his paternal sire had invented the steamboat and so maintained, though he was punished for it in school, when it was sought to teach him that Robert Fulton was the steamboat inventor." Afterward, the John Fitch Chapter DAR, under the direction of Mrs. Henry Muir, hosted a luncheon for the 65 "especially invited guests" at the Sweete Shoppe.

The Vermont granite monument is 16 feet high, weighs 40 tons, and rests on a concrete base. Fitch's remains were re-interred in the sarcophagus underneath the monument. Mrs. Johnson expressed great satisfaction in achieving this goal, but said, "Now we must work to have the history books corrected to show that John Fitch was the real inventor of the steamboat."

The Great Depression and Prohibition were two strikes against the economy in Nelson County. Highway Commissioner Ben Johnson, local politician, set in motion many new road projects in the years between 1930 and 1935. These improvements provided jobs and contributed to tourism.

In 1926, the Old Kentucky Home Commission organized a birthday celebration for Stephen Collins Foster on July 4 at the Federal Hill plantation. In the 1930s, this event was revived by Mrs. Robert Vaughn of Glasgow, a new member of the commission. She led others in planning and organizing an affair that drew people from all over the state. In 1932, a mile-long parade, picnicking on the grounds, mass-singing at the natural amphitheater in front of the house, and political speakers were the planned program. Local civic groups took responsibility for the clay pigeon shoot, dance, and state Drum and Bugle Corps contest. Drenching rain at midday hurt the event at the home until WHAS radio moved their broadcasting equipment inside the hallway and broadcast a piano rendition of Foster's songs instead of the performance of musical groups from state colleges. But Senator Alben W. Barkley continued the program and spoke of Kentuckians' pride in their state.

Immediately after this successful celebration, plans were made for 1933. Not wanting to repeat picnicking in cars and rain-drenched singing, a pavilion was built to accommodate 600 people at a cost of $5,000. At the east end of Market Street, the new "monster state highway fill" was completed, and was used by traffic and the 5-mile-long parade. The report of 10,000 people attending and 2,600 vehicles parked on the park grounds gives some idea of the attendance. The natural amphitheater in the front of the home was filled with 3,000 people singing Foster melodies for the radio broadcast by WHAS. An invitation to "Come Home" was issued to the sons and daughters of Nelson County who lived away.

In 1935, a different focus was sought by the organizers. Historic dress, mule- and horse-drawn old buggies and farm wagons, historic scenes on floats, old dances in the open air pavilion, and historic vignettes to bring back memories of Foster's time were sought. A dramatization of John Rowan meeting Henry Clay, disembarking from a coach and leading him to a card table under a shade tree to indulge in their weekly game of cards, was a hit with the visitors. Choral groups and bands from Western State College and Louisville School of Music entertained the crowd sitting under the trees in the valley below the home when everyone joined in the "mass sing." Times were hard in Nelson County as they were throughout the nation during this, the Depression, but Bardstown's Foster Days were celebrations of homecoming and music enjoyed by Kentuckians and Americans by way of radio.

"After seventeen dry years legal liquor is flowing again in Nelson county, ancient stronghold of Kentucky whiskies." Issues of *The Kentucky Standard* from 1934 until 1937 reveal the reopening of the whiskey industry in the Nelson County area after repeal in December 1933.

On March 1, 1934, the newspaper reported that the reconditioned Clear Springs plant had been renamed the Bardstown Distillery. W.O. Stiles and Charley Neuman were partners in the operation. On May 17, they announced that they would "double its capacity to 600 bushels and will run to July 1st."

On March 8, 1934, the story was that H. McKenna, Inc. (at Fairfield) was second in the county to resume operation. They enlarged the plant to handle 200 bushels of grain a day. The McKenna brand didn't lapse during Prohibition, as it was manufactured at a Louisville distillery for medicinal purposes. Coleman Bixler, the distiller, used some of the same yeast that was used when the distillery was closed. It was kept in a copper jug during all that time, and was tested and found to be useable. This was the first liquor to flow since 1917.

On May 5, 1934, it was reported that T.W. Samuels Distillery, at Deatsville, had their initial run of whiskey. It was the third distillery to resume operation. It was an entirely new plant built adjacent to the railroad (the old plant was down the road toward Lenore) and consisted of one warehouse of 10,000 barrels, a cistern house, a power house, a drying house, modern machinery, and practically every up-to-date facility used in the manufacture of whiskey. Morgan Edelen was the distiller, having worked as a distiller for Samuels since 1899. L.B. Samuels was vice president and general manager. His son T.W. Samuels was also associated with the distillery.

On August 30, 1934, the newspaper highlighted that the S.P. Lancaster Distillery was being rebuilt on the old site.

On September 8, 1934, it was reported that the Tom Moore Distilling Company completed its plant on the former site and ran its first whiskey into barrels on the day the article was published. The new plant had a capacity of 1,000 bushels a day. "In many cases the whiskey was sold as rapidly as made with no opportunity to store any of the product for aging purposes." This was the third bourbon and rye plant to open. The first run was Tom Moore, but Woodcock and Rosebud were also manufactured. The production of the rye whiskies, Tom Moore, Monteagle, and Hazelwood was planned. In the summer of 1935, the plant closed for six weeks in order to install a cooling system. In the year after

Bemis Allen stands in front of Federal Hill in the early 1930s. He greeted and entertained visitors with tales of being the son of "Old Black Joe." The drive visible in front of the home was used by all visitors until the 1950s when a new entrance was built.

reopening, thousands of barrels of whiskey were manufactured and shipped to California, New Orleans, Atlanta, New York, Chicago, Pittsburgh, and many other parts. The capacity was doubled and the pace was so fast that "all slop was given away free to those who came for it."

An article on November 19, 1936 stated that C.P. Moore was general manager at International Distilling Corporation at Arvada, Colorado. L.C. Shircliff, who worked at Early Times for 24 years and at Waterfill and Frazier Distillery in Mexico for two years as a master distiller, was in charge of the 1,000 gallons of daily production. This distillery began operation in 1934. "Until a few months ago he (Moore) was a large stockholder in Tom Moore."

On March 28, 1935, it was reported that the James B. Beam Distillery at Clermont had just completed the first run of whiskey on March 25. They produced five brands, including Old Tub, F.G. Walker, Five Beams, Cave Hollow, and Colonel James B. Beam. Five Beams referred to Jacob Beam, David Beam, J.H. Beam, J.B. Beam, and T.J. Beam, all identified with the manufacture of fine whiskies during the history of whiskey-making in Kentucky. The plant was located on the old site of Murphy, Barber and Company. A lake was constructed to supply sufficient water. The dam for the lake was produced by the dumping of strippings from the quarries of the Sunbeam Quarry Company operated for the past several years by James B. Beam and his son T.J. Beam.

On August 1, l935, it was noted in the newspaper that Old Heaven Hill Distillery was incorporated with capital stock of $50,000. Ground was leased from

When Heaven Hill distillery was built in 1935, Joe Beam was the master distiller and helped Joe Brant, the architect, to plan the buildings. H.D. Shain, distillery superintendent, was in charge of construction, Gary Shapira was president, and Ed Shapira was general manager.

William J. Smith, Mrs. Mary Jones, and Mrs. Lettie Jones. Work was started on the plant at once. It had a capacity of 200 bushels a day. The investors were M.P. Muir, Joe L. Beam, R.J. Nolan, and Gary Shapira. (A later story called it Heaven Hill Springs and indicated that Gary Shapira was president and Ed Shapira was general manager.) Joe Beam was the master distiller and helped Joe Brant, the architect, to plan the buildings. H.D. Shain, distillery superintendent, was in charge of construction.

On September 26, 1935, it was reported that the Cummins Distilling Corporation, the owners and operators of the old J.M. Atherton Distillery in LaRue County, started production on August 13 after being shut down for 17 years. It was new and complete in every detail. Since opening, the orders were so great, they doubled the mashing.

On January 25, 1936, the newspaper said that the Old Greenbrier plant was purchased by W.O. Stiles and J.F. Conway from Chicago capitalists in the spring of 1935. The partnership of Conway, Leo Smith, and C.E. Keith constructed a plant and warehouse at Greenbrier, Kentucky on the site of the famous old distillery of that name. It was located 6 miles east of Bardstown on the L&N Railroad.

On May 28, 1936, the newspaper stated that six structures were to be erected at once by the Fairfield Distillery Company. Walter C. Wagner, architect and engineer, was supervising the erection of a still building, fermenting house, power plant, government office, 10,000-barrel warehouse, and a bottling plant. Three months later, the plant went into production. An ironclad, 20,000-barrel warehouse was waiting for the 600-bushels-a-day production of 60 barrels of whiskey. President S.L. Guthrie announced Guy Beam as chief distiller and Pride Of Nelson the featured product.

On September 24, 1936, it was reported that the Willett Distilling Company was building a plant on the Loretto road with Thompson Willett as president, Mary T. Willett as vice president, and John L. Willett as secretary. John L. Willett was also the designer and engineer of the new plant. Lambert Willett, father of Thompson and John L., was the superintendent of Bernheim Distillery in Louisville.

On January 28, 1937, the Ohio River and all its tributaries were out of their banks. Nelson County rallied to the 1937 flood emergency. For the next two weeks, more than 10,000 people were fed as they passed through Bardstown to shelters in Nelson County and towns further south. The local Red Cross, operating out of the city hall building, organized housing for 1,200 refugees in the homes, schools, and churches of Bardstown and Nelson County.

Two-thirds of Louisville's inhabitants were evacuated. For a time, U.S. 31E was the only road open south of Louisville and it was closed for 24 hours by back water covering the highway north of the Salt River Bridge. Earlier in the week, the road from New Haven to Athertonville was covered. The receding waters along the river bottoms left a "countless number" of dead livestock, but it also left topsoil, the only good thing to come out of the flood.

7. ANSWERING THE CALL, 1940–1960

World War II, the Korean War, building the hospital, dealing with crime, and producing an outdoor musical were all challenges for Bardstown during this 20-year period.

In the fall of 1941, Nelson County was already in a state of war readiness. President Roosevelt called up 60,000 national guardsmen in September 1940. Four months later, the local 113th Ordinance Company was activated and 31 enlisted men and 7 officers went to Camp Shelby, Mississippi for 12 months of training. In the winter of 1941, 72 Nelson County men organized into a State Guard unit. On May 29, the nation was placed on war footing with a commitment to give every possible assistance to Britain. Local men were being drafted for the armed services and others volunteered.

Several Nelson County servicemen were reported missing or killed in the bombing of Pearl Harbor. The final number was not clear. Food rationing and government-controlled commerce were announced. The county draft board was directed to register 1,350 men between 20 and 44 years of age for potential military service. Civilians also registered for home defense as firefighters, air raid wardens, nurses, and first aid workers.

On the homefront, the Red Cross organized women to knit mufflers, vests, and navy watchcaps with government-supplied yarn. The Red Cross also organized blood drives, using a mobile unit for the first time.

In April 1942, Governor Keen Johnson asked Kentuckians to pledge that "I will Take Good Care of the Things I Have" as the motto of life during this war. Shortages were immediate and widespread. A *Kentucky Standard* editorial directed, "Accept rationing with a smile. Women repair, save and reuse clothing, darn and patch again. Toilet soap, toothpaste, and deodorant will be in short supply."

Rationing quickly affected all aspects of life. One member of each household was to register for all and receive the ration books. Books of coupons or stamps were issued for the different items and were only good for a stated period of time. Tires were rationed first, starting in December 1941. New tires were available only to essential vehicles. Used and recapped tires were in great demand. Gasoline was rationed at 3.7 gallons a week, enough to drive 2,880 miles a year. Diesel oil and kerosene were also limited. Sugar was allotted at 1 pound per person per week

A moment in time on Main Street was captured on an August day in 1940. Losson's Restaurant and Old Kentucky Home Sweete Shoppe are on the left, and the Crystal Theater is on the right. Casual jay-walkers were caught in the middle of the street.

in the spring of 1942, but raised slightly within two years. In February of 1943, every man, woman, and child was allotted stamps good for three pair of new shoes a year. Shoppers had to juggle ration stamps at the grocery, choosing coffee, canned vegetables, fruit, cheese, butter, or meat, according to the number of points you had available to spend. In 1943, meat, fish, and cheese were rationed.

In Food for Victory drives, every able-bodied student and teacher was asked to make themselves available for farm work during the summer vacation. Community canneries were opened in the summer of 1943 in Bardstown and Bloomfield to meet the goal of "every home in county to store enough food materials to run the family through winter." The Nelson County school system provided the basement of the unoccupied "new consolidated school" on Muir Avenue in Bardstown for a cannery. The Bardstown school system bought a steam boiler to be used at the site. The first foods canned came from the community garden grown on 9 acres adjacent to the Consolidated school and 2 acres at Fairfield Distillery on Bloomfield Road. In 1943, 20,000 cans of vegetables were canned for use at school lunchrooms in Boston, St. Catherine at New Haven, Chaplin, Bloomfield, and Cox's Creek. Everyone raised a garden and shared the labor and gasoline to go to the canneries.

Households were asked to save household grease to take to the butcher shops. "One teaspoon of grease will fire 5 machine gun bullets, even with rationing you

This newspaper headline tells it all. Iron fence, tin cans, old pianos, cast iron bath tubs, and broken farm machinery was gathered and weighed for the final total of 135.5 pounds per person in the county.

can save that much each day." An advertisement begged farmers for their dead stock: "Let your dead stock help to win the war." Fat, hide, and other parts were rendered and used for war products.

Students pulling wagons and baby carriages went door to door asking for old papers, envelopes, wrapping paper, magazines, letters, and cardboard. Local mailman J.B. Applegate collected more than 200 tons of paper on his own during the war years.

Rubber caps, clothing elastic, jar lids, waterproof pads, overshoes, gloves, and auto tires, 86,000 pounds in all, were gathered in a two-week drive in the summer of 1942, equaling 4,110 pounds per 1,000 people and was the third highest amount in the state. Ladies gave their old silk and nylon hose to be remade into powder bags and parachutes. One ton of steel can be derived from 9,000 tin cans, since 99 percent of the can is steel. "Take the label and the ends off and stamp flat. Leave them by the curb on the announced days."

In the spring of 1942, it was reported that "spring cleaning is ideal time to gather the metal, rubber, motor parts, plumbing fixtures, radiators, ice trays, door knobs, hinges, etc. needed to win this war. Scrap iron shortage serious, some mills are closing and don't collect any more paper."

In October 1942, all groups united to raise the Nelson County Scrap Quota of 1,800,400 pounds, or 100 pounds per capita. "Lack of Scrap may Lose the War" was the editorial. Between October 12 and October 31, civic groups, county road employees with trucks, individuals, and Boy Scouts combed the county for metal.

Old iron fences were cut down, metal roofing, cast iron tubs, pianos, radiators, broken farm machinery, any and everything of metal was gathered and tallied for the final total of 2,403,228 pounds, or 133.5 pounds per person.

As early as the summer of 1942, Nelson Distilleries was producing high wine for conversion into alcohol for use in the manufacture of smokeless powder, synthetic rubber, plastics, and medicine. Shawhan, Old Heaven Hill, and Tom Moore were already in production. Willett, Country Distillers at Deatsville, Wathen Brothers, Fairfield Distillery, J.T.S. Brown, Bardstown Distillery, and Bluegrass Distillery at Gethsemane were gearing up. The plants operated 24 hours a day for more than 3 years, producing alcohol at 150 proof. The headlines of August 3, 1944 read, "Distillers are making rye whiskey for the first time in two years." No bourbon whiskey was made because of the restriction placed on the use of corn. Eleven months later, the government had run out of storage for alcohol in favor of munitions and allowed the distilleries to produce 1 million gallons of whiskey in July.

Shortages halted city improvements. Police were instructed to enforce the vagrancy law. Mayor Conway said, "the Slogan of the Council is Fight, Work or go to Jail." Social life continued with movies, picnics, dances, and club meetings, but there were wartime reminders and restrictions. Civic clubs served meals and sponsored entertainment for visiting soldiers from Fort Knox. Long distance telephone calls were restricted, overseas packages and mail were limited, and a black-out ordinance was passed by the city council. Unnecessary lighting of store windows, street lights, outdoor decorations, or private residences was prohibited by order of the government. No Christmas lights until after the war!

Each month, the Induction Board was notified of the number to call for induction. More were called than needed because some did not pass the physical examination. First called were the young single men. By September of 1943, all of the pool of single men and married men who were not fathers had been depleted. In October 1943, 18 non-fathers and 6 fathers went for induction. By January 1944, 32 fathers were included in the draft quota, several with four or more children. In February, one dad of eight children was called for examination. By this time, the farmers in the 18-26 age group were reclassified. It was reported that 1,360 Nelson County men were serving through induction. An unknown number of other men and women had enlisted and 38 members of the 113th Ordinance Company were also serving. In the summer of 1944 it was stated that almost 10 percent of the residents of Nelson County were serving in the armed forces.

The January 13, 1942 newspaper listed 13 as having given the supreme sacrifice. On August 2, 1945, an editorial estimated that between 40 and 50 young men had given their lives. Several local soldiers were killed in the last weeks of the conflict, some in non-military plane crashes and vehicle accidents. Seventy-five servicemen from Nelson County died in World War II.

In 1943, a liberty ship was named for the late Marie Mattingly Meloney, a native of Bardstown and noted journalist. She had been decorated numerous times by the governments of France, Belgium, and Poland for her relief work among impoverished people in World War I. Charles A. Wickliffe and J.C.W. Beckham were also honored with ships named for them.

On Tuesday, August 14, 1945, wild crowds filled the streets, horns blew, the fire siren sounded, and church bells rang for more than an hour when word was received of the surrender of Japan. Men shot their rifles and shotguns into the air, others used firecrackers to celebrate. Local musicians gathered at the courthouse and Nelson Countians were dancing in the streets. (A premature celebration on Sunday night set off the siren and horn blowing until it was learned it was a false alarm.) Two days later, the gas ration was lifted and two weeks later, tourist traffic was on the upswing.

In the fall of 1945, the Sisters of Charity of Nazareth proposed to build a 70-bed hospital in Bardstown at a cost of $250,000. A design was unveiled and a 1945 fund drive was somewhat successful. Government support of hospital construction was available by 1948 and the local fund drive was continued. The ground was broken on September 12, 1949 and construction began on the $199,244 building. The official opening for patients was January 8, 1952, but a public Open House on New Year's Day was planned. Two thousand people visited the new facility and expressed approval and surprise at the well-equipped facility. On January 7, Archbishop John A. Floersh officiated at the Blessing of Flaget Memorial Hospital, named in honor of the first bishop, Benedict Joseph Flaget.

But even before the hospital was officially open, five babies were born on Sunday, January 7. On April 1, Dr. Keith Crume reported to the local Kiwanis Club that the hospital had admitted 352 patients in 3 months, with 72 births and 90 surgical cases. At Flaget Memorial Hospital, on May 31, Patti Annette, baby daughter of Mrs. Paul Mouser, became the 4,000th baby delivered by Dr. J.I. Greenwell of New Haven. He had started practicing in 1900 with horse and buggy. Now in his 50th year of practice, he liked having this hospital just "15 minutes away."

Polio—this five letter word struck fear in the hearts of Nelson County mothers in the summer of 1950. Each year, one or two cases of this dreaded disease seemed to crop up in the county, but 1950 was a different story. That year, 44 cases of polio were diagnosed. Polio is a virus that attacks and may destroy some of the nerve cells of the body. Once destroyed, they can never be replaced and paralysis is the result. Polio weakens limbs, paralyzes muscles, and threatens the ability to breathe. Left untreated, it can be deadly. There was no cure, but prompt treatment could help the body overcome the effects. Every time a child complained of a headache or had a runny nose, a trip was made to the closest doctor.

On November 13, 1952, when Reverend Joseph Howard French opened church for Mass, he was met with a scene of desecration. Saint Joseph Cathedral had been robbed of its paintings. Empty frames, some still hanging on the wall, others lying on the floor, and ladders leaning against the walls, told a tale of organized theft. One frame had fallen, damaging a radiator, and it was surmised that the noise frightened the robbers enough to leave without taking all the paintings. Early Mass-goers were horrified at the destruction and wept at the scene.

Marks in the sanctuary revealed that there were attempts to take the large painting of the Crucifixion hanging over the altar and other paintings in the sanctuary. Another painting was slightly cut. Fourteen-foot-long ladders from the school construction project next door were used to reach the paintings, which were 18 feet above the floor. Reverend James H. Willett said he had never feared a robbery because it would take very tall ladders hauled in a truck to reach the paintings. He indicated that the thieves must have had some familiarity with the construction and the cathedral.

Local police called in the state police and FBI investigators, who searched for clues. Reverend Willett indicated that the paintings were insured, but not the amount of insurance. The masterpiece paintings stolen were "The Flaying of St. Bartholomew," "The Coronation," and "The Descent of the Holy Ghost." Two paintings by American artist Jacob Hast, "St. Anne" and "The Blessed Virgin," along with four pictures portraying the Stations of the Cross, were also stolen.

The FBI arrested 11 for theft of valuable art treasures. Four of the nine paintings were discovered in the trunk of a car belonging to Norton Kretske, former assistant U.S. district attorney, in a parking lot on the north side of Chicago. Kretske was arrested on the spot. Six men were seized in Chicago, four in Ohio, and one in Pennsylvania. The paintings were recovered in good condition except for the

This was the front view of Flaget Memorial Hospital in 1951. A wing extended south creating an L-shaped building. Remodeling and additions in 1971 and 1992 changed the size, shape, and entrances of this building.

frayed edges from being cut from the frames. It would be some time before they were rehung on the walls because of the necessary restoration and repair.

All the paintings were kept until the trial was over. Former Assistant U.S. District Attorney Norton T. Kretske and former Chicago Municipal Court bailiff Joseph DePietro were indicted for receiving stolen paintings valued at $675,000. Charges against three of those first arrested were dropped for insufficient evidence. The five other paintings were recovered in Chicago by an unidentified buyer.

The value of the paintings was challenged because if they were less than $5,000, the case would not be tried in the federal court. Kenneth Donahue, an art expert and evaluator, was the government's witness. He testified that the four paintings had a value of between $9,925 and $9,950. He went on to say that "The Flaying of St. Bartholomew" was painted by a man named Maria Preti (1613–1699) and was valued at $7,500. Donahue placed a value of $1,500 on the "The Crowning of the Blessed Virgin," which was painted by an unknown painter in southern Italy.

Kretske was found guilty of having stolen paintings in his possession. He appealed and eventually went free. Arrangements were made to have the paintings returned and they arrived in Bardstown in a wooden crate in November 1957. Four paintings of the Way of the Cross were repaired and hung in February 1958.

"The Flaying of St. Bartholomew," painted by the Italian artist Maria Preti (1613–1699), was one of the paintings cut from the frames and taken from the cathedral in November 1952. It was a gift from Francis I of Sicily in the 1820s.

In July 1957, Bardstown native Mrs. Catherine Conner, director of hospitality for Kentucky, proposed the idea of a musical outdoor drama based on Stephen Foster's life to be performed at the Old Kentucky State Park. The Bardstown Chamber of Commerce picked up the ball and started the organization and drive, which resulted in "The Stephen Foster Story."

It was proposed that the state build the amphitheater, and the University of Kentucky would produce the show. Bardstown's contribution would be a $50,000 sustaining fund, part of the estimated $250,000 total cost. Paul Green, noted author of "Wilderness Road," playing at Berea, was hired to write the drama. Ted Cronk, manager of "Wilderness Road" at Berea, was hired to be coordinator and business manager of the project, with his salary paid by the state.

The amphitheater was to be built on the state park grounds, and would seat between 1,000 and 1,500 people. The show ran in July and August, and a 3-year-run was guaranteed. A nationwide search for Stephen Foster was started. Cronk reported that the state would construct the $150,000 amphitheater and lease it to the University of Louisville (U of L), which would produce the play. It was estimated that the performances would draw 55,000 admissions each year.

But U of L turned down the role of producer. A proposal that the business people of Bardstown produce the show was favorably discussed and a local non-profit body was formed to produce the drama. In February 1958, it was announced that the completion of the amphitheater could not be assured by opening night of July 4, so the project was set back a year. Cronk worked for the state parks system while waiting for the project to resume.

On July 4, 1958, the cornerstone for the amphitheater was laid and the Sundbloom painting of Stephen Foster was unveiled at the home. Six months later, the construction contract was let to Henry A. Steilberg of Louisville for $97,150. This was $22,000 more than had been allotted by the legislature, but Governor A.B. Chandler saved the day when he dipped into his emergency funds.

Then, the Governor's Commission on Tourist Promotion withdrew their pledge of $50,000. The Drama Association had to raise $40,000 to produce the show. Pledges were solicited, money was borrowed, and the Bardstown community again came forth to save the production.

Governor A.B. "Happy" Chandler named the amphitheater for his local supporter and longtime political figure, the late J. Dan Talbott, but credit was given at the end of the first season to Lieutenant Governor Harry Lee Waterfield as the man most responsible for the building of the amphitheater. Talent was solicited from throughout the United States.

In March, 400 applicants auditioned in 21 states with 100 chosen for the final test on Sunday, March 15 for the 40 roles in the drama. Seventy actor-singers made up the cast. The community was again asked for help when the stage designer needed furniture of Empire or Victorian design for the stage settings. Housing for the performers and sleeping accommodations in private homes for visitors were sought. The first performance, on June 26, was preceded by a grand parade.

"TEAMWORK DID IT!" read the lines in an advertisement in recognition of the cooperation of the Drama Association, community, county, and state efforts, which brought this grand show to Bardstown. In August, the community was stricken with the news of the sudden death of Ted Cronk on August 13. He had been involved from the very first proposal two years before. The cast carried on in the finest tradition of the stage. Visitors attended the production from every state except Nevada and Alaska. The final report of the first season showed total gross receipts of $198,789 with 65,293 paid attendance. Souvenir programs ran out three weeks before the end, which was unheard of in outdoor performances. "The Drama" was off and running and continued into the next century.

"The Stephen Foster Story" was performed in an 1850s setting under the stars. Professional singers and performers, pictured here in 1994, continue the colorful, music-filled review of Foster's career that started in 1959.

8. Important Small-Town Events, 1960–1980

Vietnam losses, President Jimmy Carter's visit, sports championships, and new industries were the leading stories of these years. In 1968, a Historic Zoning ordinance was passed to preserve Bardstown's physical heritage. Bardstown was the second community in the state to legislate preservation. More than 300 buildings were surveyed and listed on the National Register of Historic Places.

Front-page headlines in *The Kentucky Standard* on March 15, 1962 announced astonishing sports news: the Bloomfield High School basketball team was going to the state tournament! They played Taylor County. The following was reported:

> Taylor County had taken a 71-70 lead on a jump shot by Clem Haskins with 30 seconds left in the game. Bloomfield got the ball and was trying for one last shot. With only two seconds on the clock Bill Keeling connected on a close shot from the side to give Bloomfield the one point victory and title.

On the game day, the community of Bloomfield closed businesses at noon and Nelson County schools closed all day. Headlines read, "Indians Tripped in State Meet in Overtime Thriller." Favored Breathitt County had a hard time with the Indians. The score was tied nine times in regulation play. Bobby Perkins scored in the last 8 seconds to tie the score at 47-all and send the game into overtime. But in the overtime, Tommy Turner of Breathitt County was fouled by Donald Colvin and made the one-and-one for the lead at 49 to 47. The final score was Breathitt 51, Bloomfield 48.

The Bardstown Tigers football team met the 11th ranked, unbeaten Garrard County team on their home field in Lancaster, Kentucky as a 10-point underdog and vaulted into the semi-final round of the State Class A Tournament. On November 10, 1967, Coach Garnis Martin's team took an 8-1-0 record into the game, having lost to Frankfort in their first game.

They met Tompkinsville at the Bardstown Field on November 17. It didn't take long to see that Donnie Rogers's speed and the Tiger defense was going to overcome the heavier Bears of Tompkinsville, as Rogers out-raced everyone on the first offensive play to score. After beating Garrard County, described as "the toughest opponent all season," the Tigers took Tompkinsville in stride with a final score of 42 to 13.

Bardstown then faced the Mt. Sterling Trojans in Louisville on November 24 for the Class A title. The town strung banners across the streets and decorated store windows and yards. Merchants ran advertisements in support of the team with more photos of the last two games. The fans streamed to Louisville to support their team in rainy, nasty weather. These same fans must have been shaken when their team was behind 13-0 in the second quarter, but quarterback Alan Bottom passed twice to his favorite target, end Phil McKay, for a touchdown with seven minutes left in the first half. The defensive play of the team held the Trojans to only two touchdowns and a final score of 20 to 13. Toast of the town!— a new name for Coach Garnis Martin. The city of Bardstown received statewide recognition and publicity in the three weeks of the Tigers' trip to the top.

Nelson County was dealing with overcrowded schools, limited job opportunities, and transportation needs when the first reports were printed about Nelson Countians in Vietnam. Soldiers were reported as serving, but the reality of sacrifice for freedom didn't hit home until the winter of 1966. Specialist Fourth Class Raymond S. Ford, Bardstown, was the first Nelson Countian killed in combat. In March 1968, Private First-Class William David Price was reported as the third Vietnam fatality. It would be one month later when the call came that changed the lives of many Nelson County residents.

"Call Up of Bardstown National Guard Battery Will Take Many Family Men" read the headlines on April 18, 1968. Before the newspapers were read, most people in the community knew what was going on. Friends, family, and fellow workers had been called into full-time military service. Battery C, 2nd Howitzer Battalion, 138th Field Artillery of Bardstown was included in the 24,500 reservists called to active duty. The 120 men of the unit were to report on May 13. In 1965, they were evaluated as best in the state at Fort Campbell after two weeks of active training. Assigned to Fort Hood, Texas, the officers prepared the paperwork and organized the move. The men trained on new howitzers and other armament at Fort Hood. The word finally came that they were to ship out to Vietnam on October 24. A 30-day leave allowed them to move their wives back home and visit their families. During this time, the business community gathered used refrigerators, chain saws, washers, and an ice machine. Vietnam veterans advised the soldiers to take these appliances to make life easier overseas.

In early 1969, several of the men whose enlistments were up came back home. Meanwhile, accounts of three regular servicemen's deaths were reported.

"Bardstown Guardsman Killed, Two Missing, and Others Wounded as Artillery Unit Hit" was the June 26 headline. Horrified at the news and searching for more information, the families of the guardsmen called each other. It was true, Tomahawk Base had been over run by Viet Cong on June 19. The final story was told with the headlines on July 3: "Heavy Losses to Bardstown Based National Guard Unit. Mourned as Bodies Come Home for Final Rest."

146

The National Guard Unit was called up to go to the Vietnam War in 1968. Battery C of the 138th Artillery, Kentucky National Guard poses here with their flag. The third Nelson County National Guard unit to be called to federal service, they were the only unit to suffer loss of men.

Five guardsmen were killed, eleven wounded. While the community tried to comprehend this tragedy, a Lenore family was notified that their son Specialist Fourth Class Barry N. Thompson was killed on June 25.

"NELSON COUNTY HONORS ITS WAR DEAD AS NATION SYMPATHIZES." As many as 800 people attended the service to honor 11 men, 9 from Nelson County and two other members of Company C, 2nd Howitzer Battalion, 138th Artillery who died in Vietnam. Of the 110 guardsmen who left together for war a year before, 5 lost their lives in the attack on "Tomahawk Hill" on July 19. In the same building that two years before witnessed a ceremony honoring the Vietnam veterans of Nelson County, the July 4 ceremony and wake was a time to ponder the cost of the freedom that was celebrated on this day each year. National television news teams, national magazine correspondents, and the curious covered the memorial service in Bardstown.

On the morning of October 11, 3,000 people gathered in Louisville to greet the returning National Guard units. It was in the second aircraft at 7:33 a.m. that the Nelson County-based soldiers returned. Of the 386 returning troops, 65 were members of Battery C. It was time now to go home and take up where they left off 18 months before. They came home to families, a community, and a life that would forever be changed by their tour in the war that was never declared.

By the 1950s, growth of the city of Bardstown had made the three reservoirs and water from the Beech Fork River inadequate. For many years, drought conditions necessitated water conservation in the fall and winter months.

Mayor W.G.A. Sympson and the city council began applying in 1958 for assistance from federal and state governmental agencies. Political support in Frankfort and continued lobbying resulted in the construction of a new highway fill, which dammed Buffalo Creek west of Bardstown. This also eliminated a dangerous stretch of highway.

President Jimmy Carter is shown here on Main Street. Who would have believed it? Everyone who waited hours to see and hear him, and many of those who got to shake his hand, believed it. They had a wonderful memory to share with their families.

The headlines of September 5, 1963 announced the federal grant of $361,000, half the estimated cost of $700,000 for the construction of a water treatment facility and pipeline to Bardstown. This plant was designed to treat 2 million gallons of water a day, and was expected to be started before the end of 1963 and completed in one year. The storage capacity of the system would be tripled when pipelines and improvements were completed in 1964. "If everything moves according to the planned schedule the completion will be accomplished by the end of 1964."

When Guthrie M. Wilson and his council-slate campaigned in 1965, they ran on a platform of getting natural gas service and more industry for Bardstown. Previous mayors and councils tried to purchase a gas franchise from the distributor and, when that was unsuccessful, they litigated and appealed until years had gone by and still no gas system was in place.

The community owned the electric service and wanted to own the gas service as an additional revenue producer. However, the provider, Louisville Gas and Electric (LG&E), want to have Bardstown as a retail customer rather than a wholesale one. A motion to advertise for natural gas service was passed at the first council meeting after Mayor Wilson and the new council were sworn in in January 1966. Afterwards, the franchise was awarded to LG&E in March.

"There's a gap between Versailles and Elizabethtown on the East-West tollroad system," read the article in 1960 when a petition was circulated to have a road routed through this section of the state. Since the Western Kentucky and the Eastern Kentucky Toll Roads were completed, it was evident that there was "a gap" between them. In the late 1950s, local leaders were actively writing Frankfort and soliciting promises that the town would have a new highway to replace the dangerous curves of U.S. 62 between Chaplin and Lawrenceburg. Blue Grass Parkway was the name chosen for this scenic highway that opened up Nelson County in 1966 for visitors and industry, much like the old Cumberland Gap opened Kentucky for settlement in the 1770s.

"Snow Paralyzes," read the headlines on January 13, 1977 when the report of 8 inches of snow on January 9 reflected more than a week of snow and sub-zero temperatures of 5 to 15 degrees below zero. Heavy snowfall on December 29 had caused several accidents and was still on the ground. Heavy drifts up to 5 feet in depth hampered travel. Local schools closed on December 22 for the Christmas holiday. The Nelson County school system was able to open one day and Bardstown schools opened three days before the weather closed the roads. City, county, and state crews worked double shifts to keep the roads clear. Particular attention was made to the streets around the hospital, fire station, and electrical plants. As the weather continued, concern over fuel supplies and deliveries and electric utility use brought a joint statement from the mayor and county judge. On February 3, they recommended the following fuel saving moves: all businesses cut off outside advertising lights; reduce temperatures inside plants and commercial buildings to 60 degrees; reduce consumption of energy by between 5 percent and 20 percent; reduce the work week by one day; and all homes were to be extra diligent with water and electricity use in the morning hours between 7:00 and 8:30. Postal workers struggled to deliver the mail in temperatures of 14 degrees below zero and 12 inches of snow, but the mail did go through—sometimes 3 or 4 hours late. Tire chains, tow trucks, and patience were utilized by the mailmen. Not listed under the cost, but very costly and inconvenient locally, were the frozen water lines. The frost line went as deep as 24 to 26 inches, while most water lines were 18 to 20 inches deep. At some places, the ground was frozen as deep as 30 inches. Nelson County farmers lost 5,000 cattle, calves, hogs, and newborn pigs from the cold.

The students were finally able to return to school in February. By early March, the weather had moderated. The first months of 1977 would be remembered as the "long Christmas Break."

Mayor Guthrie M. Wilson received a phone call on July 24, 1979 to get ready to host a town meeting held by President Jimmy Carter at Bardstown, Kentucky. With only one week to get ready, everyone jumped on the bandwagon to put the town's best foot forward. Working with the White House staff, who arrived here late on that day, city hall employees, summer staff at the Bardstown school system, and local volunteers spent countless hours on all the details. The air conditioned gym at Bardstown High, seating 2,000 people, was chosen as the site for the town meeting. The chamber of commerce assisted in issuing tickets for the event, ordering buttons to commemorate the occasion, and helping host the many media and journalists who arrived. Later estimates of media included more than 100 journalists. Five television stations of three major networks broadcast the visit. The President traveled to Louisville's Standiford Field on Air Force One, then came by helicopter to Samuels Field, the Nelson County airport. It took four Marine helicopters to transport his entourage to Bardstown.

"I don't believe there's ever been a finer day for Bardstown and Nelson County," Mayor Guthrie Wilson said when he greeted the President at the airport. The motorcade traveled through the downtown streets about 4:40 p.m. where an estimated 7,000 people awaited his visit. Local resident Jean Wathen, standing close to the John Fitch monument, said, "All of the sudden his car stopped, and the President got out smiling, took off his coat and began shaking hands." Half a block north of the courthouse, Carter climbed on the roof of his car (probably against the desires of his secret service men), so he could see and be seen by more people. It was a very informal move, which is registered in history through the view taken by Ron Greenwell. This photo was printed on the front page of the *New York Times* as well as *The Kentucky Standard*.

The President arrived at the high school and was enthusiastically greeted by 2,094 overheated folks, who had waited more than an hour on the 18 inches of seat allotted each ticket holder. At 5:30 p.m., President Carter was introduced to the group by Mayor Wilson. The President brought greetings from his wife Rosalynn, who said "she had never received a warmer reception anywhere than she had at Bardstown earlier this month." Carter's friendly presence and informality set everyone at ease as he spoke about energy matters and the needs of the United States. He promised "openness of government by listening to the people." Then he took questions from the audience. Questions about welfare payments, gas rationing, strip-mining laws, oil profits, and even telephone service were handled with finesse. After the one-hour meeting, he left to return to Washington, leaving Bardstown with many new friends and many exciting memories of the day a President came to town. Phone calls, letters, and newspaper clippings were received for many weeks afterward showing the worldwide exposure Bardstown received during the Carter visit.

9. Preservation and Progress, 1980–2000

Several new factories were built. Historical preservation expanded. The population grew. Fires, floods, and fame were all handled. In 1982, *U.S. News and World Report* listed Bardstown as one of the 10 nicest places to live in the United States. In 1993, Bardstown was named one of the top 100 small towns in which to live in *100 Best Small Towns in America* by Norman Crampton.

In the spring of 1979, Mayor Guthrie Wilson appointed a steering committee to plan a Bardstown Birthday Celebration in 1980. The committee had flag-design contests, wrote proposals for historic markers, wrote and published a 72-page book of 120 photos of the community, and prepared activities for the historic occasion. The official opening ceremony was held on March 23 at the Bardstown High School auditorium. Mayor Wilson gave words of welcome and introduced the guest speakers: "Lt. General Harold G. Moore U.S. Army retired and John A. Fulton, Louisville attorney, pulled at the heartstrings of their peers in recalling their youth in the late 20s and early 30s amid the simple pleasures of small town life that left this impression on them."

On March 6, Mayor Wilson presented a bronze plaque honoring the first church to be erected in Bardstown to Reverend Roy Henry of the First Baptist Church on Second Street. The Nelson County Historical Society gave an account of the history of the church, a performance of the story of "Anna," and a pot luck supper. On March 22, at the southeast corner of the court square, Carlie and Ellen Wilson, granddaughters of Mayor Wilson, unveiled the official Kentucky Historic Marker honoring the settlement of Bardstown.

The Bardstown Homecoming weekend, June 28 and 29, was a success as 10,000 people lined the streets to watch a parade of 93 units. The parade theme of "Then and Now" was carried out by floats, marching bands and organizations, antique cars, horse and pony drawn units, clowns, and others. The celebration ceremony was held at the J. Dan Talbott Amphitheater with Lieutenant Governor Martha L. Collins as the featured speaker. She began her remarks with this statement: "Bardstown is famous for its Old Kentucky Home but you're known first of all for your high degree of civic pride." That pride was evident in the great volunteers and the many hours they spent working on the celebration events. Other events included an antique farm machinery show, balloon race, community picnic, re-enactment of the Orphan Brigade Reunion of 1887, religious heritage observance program, Pioneer Christmas Bazaar, and Hanging of the Greens Christmas program. Someone commented, "This has been so much fun. Let's do it again." After the moans and groans stopped, the answer was heard: "Alright, we will—a hundred years from now."

On Wednesday evening, July 2, 1980, between 8:30 and 9:00 p.m., high winds, rain, and hail struck the community. Called "something less than a tornado" by weather officials, it acted like a tornado when it swept through the town. The unexpected storm was sighted and the warning siren sounded from the police station. Only one warning sounded before the power failed. Without a back-up generator, the siren fell silent. Trailers were flipped and ripped open. Fortunately, the occupants suffered only minor injuries. Trees swirled, whipped, and were pulled from the ground. Electricity was knocked out to more than 40 percent of the customers. The hospital fell back on its emergency generator, but had power restored by Thursday morning. Bardstown immediately hired professional electric crews to assist in the 24-hour, 5-day effort to restore power.

Mayor Gus Wilson and County Judge Charles Roberts requested the National Guardsmen, as it was soon apparent that the scope of clean-up was beyond local resources. The guardsmen cut and hauled fallen trees and debris from the blocked streets. The tallest and oldest trees in the community were snapped and lying across streets, automobiles, and yards.

Other major damage was at the Heaven Hill and Barton Distilleries. Of the 25 warehouses, 23 were hit—3 with the roofs completely torn away. Some people gave up trying to cope without electricity in the hot weather and checked into motels. The powerless groceries and convenience stores gave away frozen food.

Three weeks later, Mother Nature showed her power again when, on Sunday, July 27 at 2:52 p.m., an earthquake tremor registering 5.1 on the Richter scale was felt in Nelson County. Bardstown cleaned up and made plans for replanting the 300 trees lost in this storm. In the middle of the 200th birthday celebration of Bardstown, the citizens got a wake-up call about taking their beautiful community for granted.

At the groundbreaking ceremonies for the American Greetings plant on April 14, 1983, Mayor Guthrie M. Wilson was quoted, "the arrival of American Greetings is signaling a new period of growth for Bardstown and Nelson County." No one could have foreseen how appropriate that statement was. During the next four years, four more industries located here.

The Bardstown Industrial Development Corporation was founded in the 1960s by local businessmen to assist businesses to locate in Bardstown. The early volunteer committee successfully landed Bird & Son, Owen Illinois, and the Burroughs companies. After the initial effort slowed down, a new commitment to attract more industry resulted in a budget for a full-time director and staffed office. James H. Nutter, a former economic development specialist with the state government, was hired in July 1982.

On January 18, 1985, the $4 million Wenco plant, built across from Bird & Son in the industrial park, announced it was ready to begin production. Eighteen months after Jeld-Wen announced it would build in Bardstown, Jedico of Japan bought land in the industrial park to build a plant. Impressed with the hospitality of the people and Bardstown when he visited Kentucky, President Kyoji Kobayashi made up his mind on the spot that this was where the Jedico of Kentucky plant would be built.

The headlines of the May 21, 1986 *Kentucky Standard* announced, "Bardstown Lands Two Auto Plants." Plans were announced that Woodbridge-Inoac Incorporated would construct a $7.5 million facility to manufacture automotive instrument panels. They planned to supply parts to the Ford Motor Company in Louisville. As the growth continued, three more factories were built in the industrial park.

On November 7, 1996, Heaven Hill Distillery lost seven warehouses and the distillery to fire. These seven-story, tin-covered wooden buildings were filled with wooden barrels of whiskey. More than 20,000 barrels were in each warehouse. The Bardstown Volunteer Fire Department quickly responded to the 2 p.m. alarm and requested back up from other Nelson County stations, as well as units from

On November 7, 1996, two Heaven Hill warehouses were in flames with a river of burning alcohol rolling over the hill toward two more warehouses and the distillery. It became a 16-alarm fire with 12 different departments answering the call.

nearby counties. High winds spread the flames. It became a 16-alarm fire with 12 different departments answering the call. A heavy rain about an hour after the first alarm helped keep the flames from spreading to the dry fields, but two warehouses were already in flames with a river of burning alcohol rolling over the hill toward two more warehouses and the distillery.

Down at the distillery, the workers ran toward their vehicles parked alongside KY 49, but the flowing river of burning whiskey got to the parking lot first. The men fled back over the road and up through the woods to safety. Water would not be used on the blaze, but could be used to limit the fire. Bardstown's new 100-foot ladder truck and Okolona's ladder truck sprayed more than 1 million gallons of water from fire hydrants over two warehouses in the path of the fire. Fifteen federal investigators arrived and sorted through the rubble to determine the cause of the fire. When they left on Tuesday evening they reported that "the cause of the Heaven Hill fire is undetermined." They also commented, "This is the hottest fire our team has ever seen. Some of us have been doing this 25 years." Heaven Hill leased a distillery in Louisville and continued operation using the same starter batch of yeast used to make the firm's trademark bourbon. It had been rescued from the distillery fire.

Early on Saturday morning, March 7, 1998, smoke drifted through the streets of Bardstown, telephones rang, and many hurried to dress and actually see what

The Talbott Tavern was burning from a fire that started under the main wooden stairway. Roaring up the stairway to the roof and second floor, the flames were spreading under the different roof additions. Sixty firefighters battled the blaze. The main walls were saved and the building was restored.

was impossible to believe. The Talbott Tavern was burning. Hundreds of people lined the streets with tears in their eyes as they saw a part of history destroyed by fire. The fire began under the main wooden stairway. Roaring up the stairway to the roof and second floor, the flames were spreading under the different roof additions. Firefighters ran hoses two blocks to Broadway to tap into a newly laid, 16-inch water main. Every fire department in Nelson County contributed men and equipment. Sixty firefighters battled the blaze. They were on the site 13 hours fighting hot spots.

Concern over the spread of the fire to nearby buildings was relieved when it was evident that the firefighters had it contained. The roof, ceilings of the upper floors, and stairway were completely destroyed. Water damaged the lower areas, which were not burned. The basement was completely flooded. The building was salvageable, but the walls were standing unsupported by a roof structure. Two weeks later, the owners worked to get a temporary roof on the building, as the spring rains were adding to the damage in this roofless structure.

Restoration specialists and consultants helped review the damage and plan for the restoration. It would be 19 months before all the repairs and renovations were completed, but the Talbott Tavern quietly opened its doors again November 9, 1999. The stone and brick building on the southwest corner of the public square in Bardstown still occupies its honored place, as the old Talbott Tavern survived its closest call in its 200 years of existence.

On March 1, 1997, more than 9 inches of rain fell on Nelson County in a 24-hour period. Back water from the flooded Beech Fork River threatened the water treatment plant on U.S. 62. City workers began sandbagging around the plant when the water began to rise, but they needed help. At 1 a.m. on Sunday, an appeal for volunteer help brought out more than 80 people, who were transported to the site by school bus. Young, old, men, women, youths, Japanese, Bosnian, tourists, and natives—all worked filling sandbags and placing them around the plant to protect the clarifier pumps, but the water continued to rise and the plant was flooded.

A water supply crisis occurred with Mayor Henry Spalding proclaiming an emergency water restriction—no water except for drinking purposes. Schools closed, factories canceled shifts, the hospital brought in bottled water and canceled surgeries, stores quickly sold out of their normal supply of bottled water, and arrangements were made to haul water in from other communities. On Tuesday, after a tremendous effort of city employees, the plant was cleaned and back on-line treating water.

Shock and denial was what all Bardstown United Methodist Church members were feeling and thinking early on Sunday morning, May 24, 1998, as they looked at the charred shell of the bell tower and their fire-damaged church. A lightning strike smoldered in the tower until noticed by a policeman. The fire was contained in the upper part of the original building. Smoke and water damaged the educational section. The collapse of the ceiling over the sanctuary caused damage to the supports under the main floor. The bell was removed from the tower as its support was burned through. An encouraging sight was that all the 1890 stained glass windows were intact with the exception of the half-round section over the front door, which was broken when the flames were doused. The pulpit, chairs, and piano were salvaged, but the historic organ was too damaged. The building was repaired with a new copper roof, a new bell tower, and a new 900-pound bell, which were installed by June of 1999. The bell tower was an exact replica of the original.

These stories are just some of the highlights of the twentieth century. Many more important things happened to improve and preserve the small-town way of life in a community that was growing, industrially and commercially.

In 1780, when the first 33 settlers chose to settle in "Mr. Bard's town," they built houses, started businesses, and became involved in the growth of a town. They were challenged to overcome many hardships. Over the next two hundred years, Bardstown citizens organized and worked together, building schools, churches, public buildings, and governments. Today, 10,374 citizens of Bardstown continue to live, work, and contribute to the community, preserving history, offering hospitality, and making bourbon whiskey here in central Kentucky 220 years later.

This official Bardstown Flag was designed by Jeff Willett of Bardstown. It has a red corner with the fleur-de-lis *in gold, a white stripe with the letters in navy blue, and a navy blue corner with the settlement date of 1780 in gold. It was unveiled at the first bicentennial event in March 1980.*

BIBLIOGRAPHY

Allison, Young E. *The Old Kentucky Home*. Bardstown, KY: My Old Kentucky Home Commission Federal Hill, 1923.

An Atlas of Nelson and Spencer Counties, Kentucky. Philadelphia, PA: D.S. Lake and Co., 1882.

Collins, Lewis. *History of Kentucky*. Covington, KY: Collins and Company, 1847.

Elliot, Sam Carpenter. *The Nelson County Record*. Bardstown, KY: Record Printing Company, 1896.

Garraghan, Gilbert J.S.J. Ph.D. *The Jesuits of the Middle United States*. New York: American Press, 1938.

Hafendorfer, Kenneth A. *They Died by Twos and Tens*. Louisville, KY: F.H. Press, 1995.

Hibbs, Dixie P. *Nelson County, Kentucky A Pictorial History*. Norfolk, VA, Donning Co., 1989.

———. *Nelson County A Portrait of the Civil War*. Charleston, SC: Arcadia Publishing, 1999.

———. *The Kentucky Standard Centennial History Book*. Bardstown, KY: That Special Touch Publishing, 2001.

———. *Bardstown, Images of America*. Charleston, SC: Arcadia Publishing, 1998.

Howlett, Rev. W.J. *St. Thomas Seminary*. Cleveland, OH: Dillon/Liederbach, Inc., 1971.

Kentucky Standard, The. Bardstown, KY: Standard Publishing Co., 1900–2000.

Kleber, John E. *The Kentucky Encyclopedia*. Lexington, KY: University Press of Kentucky, 1992.

Nazareth Archives. Nazareth, KY: Sisters of Charity of Nazareth.

Nelson County Historical Society Archives. Bardstown, KY.

Smith, Sarah B. *Historic Nelson County, Its Towns and People*. Bardstown, KY: GBA/Delmar, 1983.

Spalding, Mattingly. *Bardstown, Town of Tradition*. Baltimore, MD: St. Mary's Industrial School Press, 1942.

Thomas, John B. Jr. "A History of the Civil War in Nelson County, Kentucky." Newspaper series. Bardstown, KY: Standard Publishing, 1986.

———. *A History of Nelson County Newspapers*. Bardstown, KY: Standard

Publishing, 1984–1985.

Webb, Ben J. *Centenary of Catholicity in Kentucky*. Louisville, KY: Charles A. Rodgers, 1884.

Workers of Federal Writes Project of WPA for the State of Kentucky. *Military History of Kentucky*. Sponsored by the Military Department of Kentucky, G. Lee McClain, Adjutant General. Frankfort, KY: The State Journal, 1939.

NEWSPAPERS

Bardstown Gazette. Bardstown, 1841–1860, H. Milburn McCarty.

Bardstown Herald. Bardstown, 1830–1837, D.D. Jones.

Bardstown Repository. Bardstown, 1812–1816 James Bard & Marques Barnett.

Candid Review. Bardstown, 1807–1809, Peter Isler.

The Catholic Advocate. Bardstown, 1836–1841, Bardstown, Ben Webb.

Kentucky Gazette. Lexington, KY, 1791–1811, James Bradford.

Louisville Democrat. Louisville, 1860–1865.

Louisville Journal, Louisville, 1860–1865, George Prentice.

Nelson County Record. Bardstown, 1879–1900, John P. Murray and Sam Carpenter Elliott.

The Western American. Bardstown, 1803–1806 Francis Peniston.

The Western Herald. Bardstown, 1824–1830, D.D. Jones.

The Western Protestant. Bardstown, 1836–1838, Nathan L. Rice.

Index